# Palgrave Macmillan Studies in Family and Intimate Life

Series Editors
Lynn Jamieson
University of Edinburgh
Edinburgh, UK

Jacqui Gabb
Faculty of Arts & Social Sciences
Open University
Milton Keynes, UK

Sara Eldén
Lund University
Lund, Sweden

Chiara Bertone
University of Eastern Piedmont
Alessandria, Italy

Vida Česnuitytė
Mykolas Romeris University
Vilnius, Lithuania

'The Palgrave Macmillan Studies in Family and Intimate Life series is impressive and contemporary in its themes and approaches'
– Professor Deborah Chambers, Newcastle University, UK, and author of *New Social Ties*.

The remit of the Palgrave Macmillan Studies in Family and Intimate Life series is to publish major texts, monographs and edited collections focusing broadly on the sociological exploration of intimate relationships and family life. The series encourages robust theoretical and methodologically diverse approaches. Publications cover a wide range of topics, spanning micro, meso and macro analyses, to investigate the ways that people live, love and care in diverse contexts. The series includes works by early career scholars and leading internationally acknowledged figures in the field while featuring influential and prize-winning research.

This series was originally edited by David H.J. Morgan and Graham Allan.

Helena Wahlström Henriksson
Anna Williams • Margaretha Fahlgren
Editors

# Narratives of Motherhood and Mothering in Fiction and Life Writing

palgrave
macmillan

*Editors*
Helena Wahlström Henriksson
Centre for Gender Research
Uppsala University
Uppsala, Sweden

Anna Williams
Department of Literature
Uppsala University
Uppsala, Sweden

Margaretha Fahlgren
Department of Literature
Uppsala University
Uppsala, Sweden

ISSN 2731-6440 ISSN 2731-6459 (electronic)
Palgrave Macmillan Studies in Family and Intimate Life
ISBN 978-3-031-17210-6 ISBN 978-3-031-17211-3 (eBook)
https://doi.org/10.1007/978-3-031-17211-3

This Palgrave Macmillan imprint is published by the registered company Springer Nature Switzerland AG.
The registered company address is: Gewerbestrasse 11, 6330 Cham, Switzerland

# Praise for *Narratives of Motherhood and Mothering in Fiction and Life Writing*

# CONTENTS

# NOTES ON CONTRIBUTORS

**Jenny Björklund** is Professor of Gender Studies at Uppsala University. Her current research deals with cultural representations of in/voluntary childlessness, and reproductive decision-making and climate change. Her books include *Maternal Abandonment and Queer Resistance in Twenty-First-Century Swedish Literature* (2021), *Lesbianism in Swedish Literature: An Ambiguous Affair* (2014), and, as co-editor with Ursula Lindqvist, *New Dimensions of Diversity in Nordic Culture and Society* (2016). Her work has also appeared in *Women's Studies*, *Social Science & Medicine*, *Scandinavian Studies*, and *Contemporary Women's Writing*, as well as in edited volumes.

**Margaretha Fahlgren** is a professor emerita in the Department of Literature at Uppsala University. Her research includes studies on works by Swedish authors and life writing. She was part of the project *Mother Anyway: Literary, Medical and Media Narratives* (2017–19), funded by the Swedish Research Council.

**Lisa Grahn** has a doctorate in literary studies. She wrote her dissertation on motherhood as a theme in Sara Lidman's *Railroad Epic* (1977–1999). Her research examines representations of motherhood in literature and social media, twentieth-century Swedish literature and historical novels. She is currently a lecturer in the Department of Literature at Uppsala University, Sweden.

**Christine Hamm** (f. 1971) is Professor of Scandinavian Literature at the University of Bergen. She has published books and articles on Norwegian women writers such as Amalie Skram, Torborg Nedreaas, Hanne Ørstavik and Vigdis Hjorth. Her research has been devoted to questions concerning class and gender in literature. More specifically, Hamm has explored different kinds of parents as they are described by Sigrid Undset. Hamm's book *Foreldre i det moderne: Sigrid Undsets forfatterskap og moderskapets grammatikk* was published in 2013. Recently, Hamm has worked on descriptions of precarious motherhood in Scandinavian novels.

**Valerie Heffernan** is Professor of Literary and Cultural Studies at the Maynooth University School of Modern Languages, Literatures and Cultures. Her research interests include contemporary German-language literature by women and cultural representations of motherhood. She is co-editor (with Gay Wilgus) of *Imagining Motherhood in the Twenty-first Century* (2021) and (with Gillian Pye) *Transitions: Emerging Women Writers in German-Language Literature* (2013).

**Helena Wahlström Henriksson** is Professor of Gender studies and Associate Professor of American Literature at Uppsala University. Her research interests include feminist cultural studies, studies of family and kinship, life writing, popular culture, parenting over the life course. A recent publication is "Moms, Memories, Materialities: Sons Write Their Mothers' Bodies" (*a/b: Auto/Biography Studies* 2021), and an ongoing project investigates representations of single parents in Swedish media. She was the coordinator of the Swedish Network for Family and Kinship Studies 2014–2019, and participated in the project *Mother Anyway: Literary, Medical and Media Narratives* (Swedish Research Council 2017–2019).

**Eglė Kačkutė** is Associate Professor of French and Migration Studies at Vilnius University. Her research focuses on contemporary women's writing and transnational mobilities, especially on mothering across cultural and linguistic barriers and highly educated migrant mothers. She is the author of *Svetimos ir Savos* (*Strange and Familiar*, Vilnius University Press 2012), the co-author of photo story *Portrait of a (Working) Mother* (Georg, 2019), as well as co-editor of *Transgression(s) in Twenty-First-Century Women's Writing in French* (Brill/Rodopi, 2021).

**Elizabeth Kella** is Associate Professor of English at Södertörn University, South Stockholm. Her research investigates family and community in American literature after the Second World War. In a recent project, "Remembering Poland and Eastern Europe: Nostalgia, Memory, and

Affect in Diasporic Women's Writing" she studies, *inter alia*, representations of mother-daughter relations.

**Elizabeth Podnieks** is a professor in the Department of English at Toronto Metropolitan University, Canada. Her work on parenting and caregiving has appeared in, among others, the *Journal of the Motherhood Initiative for Research and Community Involvement*, *Life Writing*, the *Encyclopedia of Motherhood*, and the *Routledge Companion to Motherhood*. She is the co-editor of *Textual Mothers/Maternal Texts: Motherhood in Contemporary Women's Literatures*; and the sole editor of *Mediating Moms: Mothers in Popular Culture*, and *Pops in Pop Culture: Fatherhood, Masculinity, and the New Man*. She is the author of the monograph *Maternal Modernism: Narrating New Mothers*.

**Anna Williams** is a professor in the Department of Literature at Uppsala University. Her research interests include nineteenth- and twentieth-century Swedish literature, gender studies and biography. She was PI of the research project *Mother Anyway: Literary, Medical and Media Narratives* (2017–19), funded by the Swedish Research Council.

# CHAPTER 1

# Ambivalent Narratives of Motherhood and Mothering: From Normal and Natural to Not-at-all

*Helena Wahlström Henriksson, Anna Williams, and Margaretha Fahlgren*

The chapters in this volume focus on contemporary (representations of) meanings of motherhood and mothering. Together, they demonstrate the significance of literary narratives for understanding, and critiquing, motherhood and mothering as social phenomena and subjective experiences.

This publication has received funding from the European Union's Horizon 2020 research and innovation programme under grant agreement No 952366, and from the Centre for Gender Research and the Department of Literature at Uppsala University.

H. W. Henriksson (✉)
Centre for Gender Research, Uppsala University, Uppsala, Sweden
e-mail: Helena.henriksson@gender.uu.se

A. Williams • M. Fahlgren
Department of Literature, Uppsala University, Uppsala, Sweden
e-mail: anna.williams@littvet.uu.se; margaretha.fahlgren@littvet.uu.se

© The Author(s) 2023
H. Wahlström Henriksson et al. (Eds.), *Narratives of Motherhood and Mothering in Fiction and Life Writing*, Palgrave Macmillan Studies in Family and Intimate Life,
https://doi.org/10.1007/978-3-031-17211-3_1

1

They all contextualize motherhood and mothering in terms of their particular national and cultural location, in analyses of texts by authors from Canada/Lebanon, Norway, Sweden, Switzerland, and the United States. They move between narratives about mothers who are firmly placed in one national context, and those who are in "in-between" positions due to migrant experiences. This opens for comparison and invites discussions about how representations of mothers, mothering, and motherhood are impacted by different national and cultural circumstances. Each chapter also explores how motherhood is textualized; that is, how tone, voice, literary style, language, structure, and genre contribute to building representations of maternal (in)experience and mothering practices. Hence, the studies in this book work in interdisciplinary fashion, to engage literary/ humanities as well as social science perspectives.

These chapters also variously demonstrate that in literature as in life, motherhood is constructed intersectionally: gender, class, race, nationality, sexuality, and age all impact upon how motherhood can be done, as do migrant experiences. Offering a diversity of critical responses and theorizations of motherhood and mothering, and drawing upon literary studies of the construction of motherhood (Bassin et al. 1994), these original analyses address a range of representations, meanwhile raising crucial questions about how motherhood and mothering are marked by absence and/or presence and by profound ambivalences, about how maternal perspectives and voices gain space or mix with filial voices in the narratives, and about negotiating ideals and norms of motherhood. The contributions draw upon a variety of theorizations of motherhood, from literary theory, cultural studies, memory studies, social science theory, gender and queer theory, and psychoanalysis. Furthermore, the chapters variously foreground and link together the themes central to this volume: embodied experience/maternal embodiment; notions of what is "normal" or natural (or not) about motherhood; maternal health and illness; mother-daughter relations; maternality and memory; and the (im)possibilities of giving voice to the mother. Hence, taken all together, the chapters in this volume offer a broad range of perspectives in terms of geopolitical places, thematic concerns, theoretical approaches, and interdisciplinary takes on investigating motherhood and mothering.

The twenty-first century is marked by often contradictory tendencies regarding mothers and mothering. Many countries in the global North— the place from which the contributors in this volume are speaking—have seen measures toward increased gender equality in terms of more equal expectations on men and women to provide childcare as well as hold jobs outside the home. This can be interpreted as a relatively lessened differentiation between the worlds of fathers and mothers. Furthermore, assisted reproductive technologies have become increasingly accessible. Assisted reproductive technologies (ARTs) separate sexuality from procreation, gestational parents from genetic parents, and social from biological parents, a development which is liberating for some and contributes to expanding contemporary definitions of parenthood far beyond the genetic/biological. Yet, in the same time period, there also seems to have been an increased idealization of "natural" motherhood and maternal instincts, and there is a new conservatism in Northern Europe that formulates motherhood as a full-time job and asks women to turn away from paid employment.

The French historian Élisabeth Badinter (2011) captures this latter tendency and theorizes it as an ongoing process that is visible in several areas of the public and private spheres. "Over the last three decades, almost without our noticing, there has been a revolution in our idea of motherhood. This revolution was silent, prompting no outcry or debate, even though its goal was momentous: to put motherhood squarely back at the heart of women's lives." Badinter puts her finger on the "resurrection" of motherhood as determining women's lives and formulates it as a form of backlash to feminist movements. Whether the idea that motherhood is "at the heart of women's lives" was ever truly dead, is, however, a matter of contention.

While it is not the goal of this volume to determine the causes behind the (simultaneous) developments outlined above, as literary scholars and gender researchers we see the need for investigating these different pulls and tendencies, how they speak to or against one another, and how they find expression in texts. Therefore, investigating definitions and practices of motherhood and mothering, as well as their effects, is a central concern of this volume. As the following chapters variously demonstrate, motherhood can indeed be understood as a "contested terrain" (Glenn et al. 1994; see also O'Reilly 2004).

As we, the editors, have undertaken this project, from our Scandinavian viewpoint, we have had reason to reflect upon differences between Swedish/Scandinavian research, and research from Europe and North America on motherhood. One reason why research on motherhood and mothering in the humanities and social sciences has not been strong in Sweden in the early twenty-first century may be the scholarly focus on masculinity and fatherhood, which has overshadowed questions about reproduction, subjectivity, and identity from the perspective of women. We contend that this is a consequence for the research of gender equality-oriented politics to strengthen the position and visibility of men as parents. In gender studies scholarship in Scandinavia, unlike fatherhood (studies), motherhood (studies) has tended to raise concerns about "biologism" and essentialism, and feminist scholars have been wary of the faulty equalization of "women" and "mothers" to the point where studies of motherhood have seemingly been avoided. However, sophisticated gender theories of bodies and embodiment and post-constructionist theory allow for new kinds of approaches to women as mothers, and to maternal bodies as lived *and* culturally encoded. At present, we see a shift toward more studies on motherhood in this location. While we are a part of this shift, we are also wary that in the currently increasingly conservative political climate in which we write this introduction, women scholars focusing of motherhood may be taken as a sign of a "natural" interest, instead of a sorely needed addition to previous literary scholarship and to family studies generally.

## MOTHERHOOD, MOTHERING, AND NARRATIVE

To say that motherhood is a gendered concept is a severe understatement. Notions of motherhood are still largely based upon the connection between woman–biology–body in relation to social functions: women, by giving birth and nursing, have supposedly natural ties with the child. The notion of the good mother is still a hegemonic discourse inherent in daily life as well as in institutional practice. This discursive construct is both explicit and implicit, creating expectations and demands that distinctively separate the situation of women as mothers from that of men as fathers.

Motherhood is a phenomenon that concerns women all around the world. This is not to say that all women mother, or are mothers, but it is to say that all women are affected in one way or another by motherhood, by its absence or presence. Furthermore, motherhood —which we take to mean the gendered situation of being a mother—and mothering—which we take to mean the gendered practice of parenting in terms of everyday care and sustenance—are ongoing day and night in all kinds of societies and environments.

As a phenomenon, motherhood is diverse and multifaceted. Already in 1997, Elaine Tuttle Hansen observed: "What is said by and about mothers—full-time mothers, surrogate mothers, teenage mothers, adoptive mothers, mothers who live in poverty, mothers with briefcases—is increasingly complicated and divisive. Language is stretched to describe the bewildering fragmentation of a time in which one child may have a genetic mother, a gestational mother, and a custodial mother, each of whom is a different person" (Hansen 1997, 1). "Mother," then, as Hansen observes, may mean many things. Motherhood is often marked by ambivalences, fraught with mixed and at times conflicted feelings, which may also change over a lifetime. All these diversities are further compounded by different power dimensions beyond gender, including class, race, nationality, sexuality, age, and ability. In the twenty-first century, debates about transgender people, and about who counts as a woman, also impact on ideas about motherhood and who can be (understood as) a mother.

But motherhood and mothering are not only defined by physical and material experiences. They also come to life through stories and recorded accounts. In narratives, in texts, motherhood gains meaning on existential and symbolic levels. On many occasions, it is these narratives, and the maternal experiences they express, whether the narratives are fictional(ized) or "documentary" that stir up debate, call attention to controversial issues and scrutinize conditions that clash with ideals and established perceptions. Among recent examples of such narratives and ensuing debates are the cases of women's stories about regretting motherhood in Israel (Donath 2017; Heffernan and Stone 2021), the voicing of maternal discontent in the UK (Cusk 2001), and a reluctance to become a mother in Canada (Heti 2018). Other examples are the debate caused by a collection of essays about life as a divorced mother in Sweden titled *Happy, happy!* (Sveland 2011), or by women choosing to be "solo" mothers (Wahlström and Bergnehr 2021; cf. Hertz 2006). What these examples have in common is that they give space to the voice of the (would-be) mother herself. The presence and absence of such perspectives in the public debate, in literary representation as such, and in what continuously takes shape as "popular culture" or the literary canon bears some scrutiny. For, while motherhood is a global phenomenon, it has yet to become an integrated part of the themes and tropes that are regularly studied in university courses in comparative literature and other relevant subjects. We therefore see the present volume as a contribution to international literary scholarship in general, as well as to "motherhood scholarship" in particular.

It is one of our fundamental points of departure for this volume that disregarding meanings of motherhood and mothering is unhelpful for feminism, since it is a experience that affects all women, as well as all men. In taking this standpoint, we are thinking with Patrice DiQuinzio's (1999) reflections on narrative and subjectivity. DiQuinzio argues that mothering is a site of contention not only in political culture but also in feminist theory. She suggests that the goals of feminist theory itself need to be reconceptualized, and argues that feminism's resistance to "essential motherhood" has led to a general erasure of motherhood as a feminist concern. With Sara Ruddick (1990), DiQuinzio emphasizes *narrativity* as central for understanding the importance of motherhood.

While it is true that motherhood and mothering take shape in narratives across many textual genres, from fictional literature to spoken narratives, from political statements to policy documents, we focus here on two main genres: first, literary fiction and second, life writing, that is, auto/biography and memoirs. The twenty-first century has seen the publication of a broad variety of fictional narratives, autobiographical writing, and essays that explore the fundamental impact of motherhood on individuals, families, and society, and taken all together, these texts do seem to constitute a "wave" of writing about maternal experience.

With its focus on literary representations, the present volume offers insights into contemporary reflections on motherhood and mothering that sometimes are part of ongoing public debates, but at other times cannot be found in public discourses. Via its typically extended narratives, literature offers the possibility to dwell upon topics that are more hurriedly abandoned in public debate and media, or that are perhaps not commonly voiced in the "first person" because they are taboo. Literature therefore is a unique source of insight into human conditions and often envisions circumstances that are as yet concealed or marginalized in society at large. It has a unique ability to convey and combine emotional, linguistic, and artistic dimensions in "storying motherhood" (Wilson and Davidson 2014). Furthermore, literary representations of mothers and mothering foreground the ways that parenthood and parenting for women are imbricated with dimensions like class, race, age, and nationality, as well as how motherhood is connected to living a heterosexual, lesbian, queer, or trans everyday life. Literature complicates questions about motherhood and non-motherhood, about norms, inclusivity, and diversity.

## RESEARCH ON LITERARY REPRESENTATIONS OF MOTHERHOOD

Literary scholarship on motherhood has been developing especially since the 1980s. Research on representations of motherhood in literature has focused on literatures of specific nations (Rye 2009; Jeremiah 2003) or geopolitical areas, as in *Reading/Speaking/Writing the Mother Text: Essays on Carribbean Women's Writing* (Herrera and Sanmartín 2015), *Motherhood in African Literature and Culture* (Akujobi 2011), and *Motherhood in Literature and Culture: Interdisciplinary Perspectives from Europe* (Rye et al. 2018). In the United States, leading African-American women writers like Toni Morrison have been intent on exploring the impact of slavery and its aftermath on motherhood and mothering, and research on their authorship, like *Toni Morrison and Mothers/Motherhood* (Baxter and Satz 2017), adds crucial dimensions to studies of motherhood in literature that also have relevance across disciplines and interdisciplines.

Feminist studies have long centered on women's writing about mothers, in fiction and in life writing. Twenty-first-century studies only rarely break this pattern, as most studies focus fictional narratives or autobiographical writing about becoming a mother from within an embodied maternal experience (Podnieks and O'Reilly 2010). Motherhood memoirs also extend further across conventional boundaries for defining "mothering" to collaborative "mother-work," as demonstrated in Elizabeth Podnieks' study of nanny narratives as "matroethnographies" (Podnieks 2021).

Feminist literary studies on motherhood in the 1980s and 1990s frequently drew upon, developed, and expanded psychoanalytic theories. E. Ann Kaplan's study of melodrama in literature and film *Motherhood and Representation* (1992/2013) is a classic in the field, which, like other crucial studies from the 1980s and 1990s such as Marianne Hirsch's *The Mother-Daughter Plot* (1989) and Elaine Tuttle Hansen's *Mother Without Child* (1997), continues to be a key reference in motherhood scholarship. Hirsch argued in the 1980s that the fundamental absence of "the maternal voice" in literature can be explained at least in part by the iteration of a general cultural disparaging of motherhood, which is also echoed by fictional protagonists. Her own focus on the mother-daughter plot and its dependence on choices regarding narrative perspective was a central contribution to motherhood studies, and a continuous focus in the research has indeed been the mother-daughter relationship. Although there are some studies of men's auto/biographical narratives about their mothers' lives as seen through the eyes of the (grown) child (Wahlström Henriksson 2021), and on male authors' fictional renditions of motherhood (Martinez 2018), these are rare exceptions to the rule. In the 2010 essay collection *Textual Mothers/Maternal Texts: Motherhood in Contemporary Women's*

*Literatures*, Elizabeth Podnieks and Andrea O'Reilly trace a development in female-authored texts about motherhood from "daughter-centric" to "matrilineal" and "matrifocal" narratives, arguing that the absent maternal voice explored by Hirsch has slowly gained ground in literature after the 1990s. They also make claims for criticism that links maternal literature closely to lived experiences, for, as they observe, "mothering and being a mother are personal, political, and creative narratives unfolding within both the pages of a book and the spaces of a life" (Podnieks and O'Reilly 2010, 2). With Podnieks and O'Reilly, the chapters in this volume show that maternal voices have entered into literary representation, full force, and that they are complicated and diverse.[1]

The research to date demonstrates that stories about motherhood are variously shaped by absences and presences, by distance and closeness. Hansen argues in *Mother Without Child* (1997) that it is above all in fiction that features "bad mothers" and mothers who lose their children that motherhood as such is questioned and scrutinized in new and potentially subversive ways. This idea is taken up in a recent study of contemporary Swedish fiction that analyzes the significance of plots where mothers leave their children, in the context of gender-equal family policy and parenting norms (Björklund 2021).

The contributions in this volume engage in dialogue with and add further dimensions to these strands of previous research: on maternal voices, the relational aspects of motherhood and mothering, and the (recent) histories of writing motherhood in literature. To speak, again, with Elaine Tuttle Hansen, we see that decades after her crucial study, "the multifaceted story of feminist thinking about motherhood is still emerging" (Hansen 1997, 10), and is likely to continue to do so as long as there are mothers, and literature that engages with motherhood and mothering.

---

[1] Symbolic meanings of motherhood, and the ways that certain tropes of motherhood circulate in a given national culture, have also been fruitfully explored in scholarship on popular culture, especially television, film, and social media. Edited volumes like *Mediating Moms* (Podnieks 2012) and *Mediated Moms* (Hundley and Hayden 2015) explore non-normative or transgressive motherhood. Film studies scholarship has scrutinized the common trope of the dead/absent mother in Anglo-American culture (Åström 2017; Devers 1998), as well as representations of both bad mothers, and struggling, heroic mothers in genre film (Arnold 2013; see also Fisher 1996; Feasey 2012). Representations of single mothers have generated separate studies (Åström and Bergnehr 2021).

## THE CHAPTERS IN THIS VOLUME

The chapters in this volume are sequenced on the basis of some major thematic concerns, although the reader will discover that there are also other overlaps between chapters and sections. The first set of studies deal with reproductive choices, sexualities, and breaking/complying with norms. A discussion of motherhood also necessitates a discussion of reproductive choices; the first study in this volume therefore raises issues around abortion as well as motherhood. Access to safe abortions continues to be a relevant issue for women all over the world, a fact that has been newly underscored by the overturning of *Roe v. Wade* in the year when we are writing this Introduction (2022). This subject is central to Lisa Grahn's chapter, "One Hand Clapping: The Loneliness of Motherhood in Lucia Berlin's 'Tiger Bites'." In Berlin's short story, a young woman travels across the Texas border into Mexico to have an abortion. Grahn shows how the depiction of the protagonist's experiences in a Mexican abortion clinic interweaves perspectives of class, language barriers, national borders, and family relationships. She argues that abortion in the short story serves to highlight the life-changing choices that surround motherhood and seems to speak for accessible safe abortions even as the protagonist herself ultimately rejects abortion. But she also links the intergenerational theme in the story to the intergenerational relevance of the story itself, across the decades from publication to present-day reading.

The concept of motherhood changes when meanings of male and female become more permeable and open-ended, as is the case in transgender lives. In "'their mothers, and their fathers, and everyone in between': Queering Motherhood in Trans Parent Memoirs by Jennifer Finney Boylan and Trystan Reese," Elizabeth Podnieks discusses the queering of motherhood in two autobiographical books from the US, Jennifer Finney Boylan's *Stuck in the Middle With You: A Memoir of Parenting in Three Genders* (2013) and Trystan Reese's *How We Do Family: From Adoption to Trans Pregnancy, What We Learned About Love and LGBTQ Parenthood* (2021). Boylan is a transgender woman, and a parent of two children, who is living in a long-term marriage. Reese is a transgender man who together with his husband adopted two children and who also gave birth to their biological child. Boylan's and Reese's accounts of their lives foreground how "mother" and "father" are concepts that are varied and mutable, while also narrated from the "conventional" framework of married life. Podnieks shows how their narratives normalize trans parenthood while queering normativity. These positions affect how they write, and Podnieks shows how their personal narratives are punctuated with community perspectives and calls for social justice.

In her contribution "Struggling to Become a Mother: Literary Representations of Involuntary Childlessness," Jenny Björklund takes her point of departure in a Swedish context. Sweden is a country with progressive family politics that encourage reproduction, and the chapter focuses on three contemporary novels that deal with women who struggle to become mothers in a political and social environment of pronatalism. In depicting an often painful and existentially challenging process, the novels serve as pertinent examples of how deeply non-motherhood is intertwined with normative femininity, heteronormativity, and traditional family ideals. The chapter examines to what extent the novels adhere to, or contest, feminine ideals of motherhood, as well as discursive Swedish gender norms and nuclear family ideals. It furthermore touches on the complex and theoretically vital question of what about motherhood is (perceived as) natural versus constructed.

From this first set of chapters that variously put pressure on definitions of motherhood and mothering, and question motherhood, we move on to the next set of chapters, which offers three studies concentrating on mother-daughter relationships, and the matter of the "mother's voice." In her chapter "Orality/Aurality and Voice of the Voiceless Mother in Abla Farhoud's *Happiness Has a Slippery Tail*," Eglė Kačkutė analyzes the 1998 novel by Lebanese-Canadian author Farhoud. Kačkutė reminds us that narratives of migrant monolingual mothers told from their own perspective are still rare in literature. The novel highlights questions of mothering in a language perceived as foreign by the children (Arabic), and being a mother in a country whose language (French) the mother does not speak. Written by the daughter but from the mother's point of view, the novel stages the mother/daughter plot by introducing the daughter as narrator—a fictionalized version of the author—in an imagined dialogue between the two where they share their Arabic mother tongue. Thus, Kačkutė argues, the novel features a double voice, a mother/daughter duet which allows for the unique specificity of each voice in their respective languages. Such narrative technique establishes a new ethics of representing other marginalized and silenced voices.

In 2020 the Jewish Swedish journalist Margit Silberstein published her autobiography *Förintelsens barn (Children of the Holocaust)*. Liz Kella's chapter, "From Survivor to Im/migrant Motherhood and Beyond: Margit

Silberstein's Postmemorial Autobiography, *Förintelsens Barn*" which continues the strand of exploring mothers and daughters begun in the previous chapter, focuses on how Silberstein represents her relationship with her mother and her strong sense of identification with the mother's past experiences. The relationship between the survivor mother and the daughter is complex and a part of the testimony of the Holocaust, and Silberstein's memoir is part of an international sub-genre of life writing by children of survivors. Questions regarding the (im)possibility of inheriting maternal memory and embodied experiences are raised in the novel, as the daughter's eating disorders are understood as a mode of identifying with and alleviating the mother's sufferings. Kella shows that the daughter's attempts to understand her mother also create an emotional ambivalence toward the female body.

A strong generation of women writers have emerged in the German-speaking countries in recent decades, offering yet other intriguing explorations of the relationship between mother and daughter. In the chapter "The (M)other's Voice: Representations of Motherhood in Contemporary Swiss Writing by Women," Valerie Heffernan observes how new and challenging perspectives on this established theme in women's literature emerged in two Swiss novels in the 1990s, Zoë Jenny's *The Pollen Room* (1998, orig. 1997) and Ruth Schweikert's *Augen zu* (1998). Heffernan demonstrates that, in different ways, the novels respond to Marianne Hirsch's call for a "double voice" in literature that makes room for the maternal perspective. By focusing on narrative form, Heffernan discerns interesting differences in the approach to the textual status of the mother's voice. In *The Pollen Room*, the daughter's anger does not make room for the mother's voice but places the narrative authority with the daughter. Schweikert's *Augen zu*, however, opens up for the double voice in letting both protagonists speak.

After these explorations of maternal voices and mother-daughter plots, we come in the final set of chapters to two studies that point to ambivalent attitudes to motherhood—in literature and in life. Meanwhile, they also variously foreground the tensions between writing and mothering, whether this is thematized in complex narratives of contemporary motherhood or evidenced by critical "misrecognition" on the part of the literary/critical establishment. During the last decade, literature about choosing not to be a mother or regretting motherhood has provoked intense discussions. In "Contested Motherhood in Autobiographical Writing: Rachel Cusk and Sheila Heti," Margaretha Fahlgren and Anna Williams discuss two contemporary autobiographical novels, which investigate women's feelings and thoughts about motherhood, Rachel Cusk's *A Life's Work* (2001) and Sheila Heti's *Motherhood* (2018). These narratives have been important in presenting alternative discourses on motherhood that have previously been rather taboo, and thereby broadening the concept as such. Both writers endeavor to understand the existential dilemma concerning motherhood by exploring their everyday experiences, and they variously reflect upon the tensions between motherhood and authorship.

The final chapter offers a perspective from Norway. In the year 2018, literary works about motherhood were published by four well established Norwegian novelists. Although very different, they all chose the novel as the literary form for exploring experiences of mothering. By close narratological analysis, Christine Hamm demonstrates in the chapter "A Plea for Motherhood: Mothering and Writing in Contemporary Norwegian Literature" how these novels address maternal experience in narratives that center on the felt need to defend the choice to be a mother. They foreground maternal experience while navigating feminist discourses as well as Norwegian family politics. The critical reception deemed these novels uninteresting and of low aesthetic quality, partly because of their subject matter and their (supposedly) auto-fictional dimensions. Hamm challenges this critical judgment, arguing that by merging fragments, essayistic pieces, memories, and reflections, the novels point to a new way of delineating the multi-layered experience of motherhood.

What these chapters taken together demonstrate is that there is diversity in the maternal voices that are emerging in fiction and life writing across national contexts in the twenty-first century. Above all, they point to the complexities and profound ambivalences of motherhood and mothering. In the words of Elaine Tuttle Hansen, "[m]otherhood offers women a site of both power and oppression, self-esteem and self-sacrifice, reverence and debasement" (Hansen 1997, 3). And, we would add, motherhood and mothering offer not just these extremes, but also the states in-between, states marked by much uncertainty and tension. These chapters also show that texts from previous decades resonate with urgent issues in our time, and that re-reading and re-thinking narratives of motherhood (and non-motherhood) "across generations" can provide inroads to understanding how representations and narration function as social critique as well as aesthetic pleasure.

REFERENCES

Akujobi, Remi. 2011. Motherhood in African Literature and Culture. *CLCWeb: Comparative Literature and Culture* 13 (1) (np).

Arnold, Sarah. 2013. *Maternal Horror Film: Melodrama and Motherhood.* Basingstoke: Palgrave Macmillan.

Åström, Berit. 2017. Marginalizing Motherhood: Postfeminist Fathers and Dead Mothers in Animated Film. In *The Absent Mother in the Cultural Imagination: Missing, Presumed Dead,* ed. Berit Åström, 241–258. Basingstoke: Palgrave Macmillan.

Åström, Berit, and Disa Bergnehr, eds. 2021. *Single Parents: Representations and Resistance in an International Context.* Palgrave Macmillan.

Badinter, Élisabeth. 2011. *The Conflict: How Modern Motherhood Undermines the Status of Women.* New York: Metropolitan Books.

Bassin, Donna, Margaret Honey, and Maryle Mahrer Kaplan. 1994. *Representations of Motherhood.* New Haven: Yale University Press.

Baxter, Lee, and Martha Satz. 2017. *Toni Morrison and Mothers/Motherhood.* Bradford: Demeter Press.

Björklund, Jenny. 2021. *Maternal Abandonment and Queer Resistance in Twenty-First-Century Swedish Literature.* Springer International.

Cusk, Rachel. 2001. *A Life's Work: On Becoming a Mother.* London: Fourth Estate.

Devers, Carolyn. 1998. *Death and the Mother from Dickens to Freud: Victorian fiction and the Anxiety of Origins.* Cambridge: Cambridge University Press.

DiQuinzio, Patrice. 1999. *The Impossibility of Motherhood: Feminism, Individualism, and the Problem of Mothering.* New York: Routledge.

Donath, Orna. 2017. *Regretting Motherhood: A Study.* Berkeley: North Atlantic Books.

Feasey, Rebecca. 2012. *From Happy Homemaker to Desperate Housewives: Motherhood and Popular Television.* London: Anthem.

Fisher, Lucy. 1996. *Cinematernity: Film, Motherhood. Genre:* Princeton University Press.

Glenn, Evelyn Nakano, Grace Chang, and Linda Rennie Forcey, eds. 1994. *Mothering: Ideology, Experience, and Agency.* New York: Routledge.

Hansen, Elaine Tuttle. 1997. *Mother Without Child: Contemporary Fiction and the Crisis of Motherhood.* Berkeley: University of California Press.

Heffernan, Valerie, and Katherine Stone. 2021. #regrettingmotherhood in Germany: Feminism, Motherhood, and Culture. *Signs: Journal of Women in Culture and Society* 46 (2): 337–360.

Herrera, Cristina, and Paula Sanmartín. 2015. *Reading/Speaking/Writing the Mother Text: Essays on Carribbean Women's Writing.* Demeter Press.

Hertz, Rosanna. 2006. *Single by Chance, Mothers by Choice: How Women are Choosing Parenthood Without Marriage and Creating the New American Family*. New York: Oxford University Press.

Heti, Sheila. 2018. *Motherhood*. New York: Henry Holt.

Hirsch, Marianne. 1989. *The Mother-Daughter Plot: Narrative, Psychoanalysis, Feminism*. Bloomington: Indiana University Press.

Hundley, Heather L. and Sara E. Hayden. 2015. *Mediated Moms: Contemporary Challenges to the Motherhood Myth*. Peter Lang.

Jeremiah, Emily. 2003. *Troubling Maternity: Mothering, Agency, and Ethics in Women's writing in German of the 1970s and 1980s*. New York: Routledge.

Kaplan, E. Ann. 1992/2013. *Motherhood and Representation: The Mother in Popular Culture and Melodrama*. London: Routledge.

Martinez, M.J. 2018. Being a Mother *Is* Insane: Cunningham's Response to Gilman and Woolf. In *A Portrait of a Lady in Modern American Literature: Poor Little Rich Girl*, ed. Aimee Pozorski. Newcastle-Upon-Tyne: Cambridge Scholars Publishing.

O'Reilly, Andrea, ed. 2004. *From Motherhood to Mothering: The Legacy of Adrienne Rich's Of Woman Born*. Albany: State University of New York Press.

Podnieks, Elizabeth. 2012. *Mediating Moms: Mothers in Popular Culture*. Montréal: McGill-Queens University Press.

———. 2021. The Synergy Between You': Mothers, Nannies, and Collaborative Caregiving in Contemporary Matroethnographies. *Life Writing* 18 (3): 337–354.

Podnieks, Elizabeth, and Andrea O'Reilly, eds. 2010. *Textual Mothers/Maternal Texts: Motherhood in Contemporary Women's Literatures*. Waterloo, ONT: Wilfrid Laurier University Press.

Ruddick, Sarah. 1990. *Maternal Thinking: Towards a Politics of Peace*. London: Women's Press.

Rye, Gill. 2009. *Narratives of Mothering: Women's Writing in Contemporary France*. Newark: University of Delaware Press.

Rye, Gill, Victoria Browne, Adalgisa Giorgio, Emily Jeremiah, and Abigail Lee Six, eds. 2018. *Motherhood in Literature and Culture: Interdisciplinary Perspectives from Europe*. New York: Routledge.

Sveland, Maria, ed. 2011. *Happy, happy. En bok om skilsmässa*. Stockholm: Atlas.

Wahlström Henriksson, Helena. 2021. Moms, Memories, Materialities: Sons Write their Mothers' Bodies. *A/B: Auto/Biography Studies* 36 (2): 1–22.

Wahlström Henriksson, Helena, and Disa Bergnehr. 2021. Reluctantly Solo? Representations of Single Others via Donor Procedure, Insemination and IVF in Swedish Newspapers. In *Single Parents: Representations and Resistance in an International Context*, ed. Berit Åström and Disa Bergnehr, 215–234. Palgrave Macmillan.

Wilson, Sheena, and Diana Davidson, eds. 2014. *Telling Truths, Storying Motherhood*. Bradford: Demeter.

# CHAPTER 2

# One Hand Clapping: The Loneliness of Motherhood in Lucia Berlin's "Tiger Bites"

*Lisa Grahn*

Access to safe and legal abortions has been a concern for generations of women, and continue to be so today. During the last 50 years, immense progress in terms of women's reproductive health has been made all over the world. However, as I began to write this piece in 2021, abortion was still heavily debated, and indeed an illegal practice, in many places. Naturally, the cultural and political discourse on the subject differs across the world. However, it is also, as Lynn M. Morgan and Meredith W. Michaels have pointed out, an issue subject to international debate,

---

This publication has received funding from the European Union's Horizon 2020 research and innovation programme under grant agreement No 952366, and from the Centre for Gender Research and the Department of Literature at Uppsala University.

---

L. Grahn (✉)
Department of Literature, Uppsala University, Uppsala, Sweden
e-mail: lisa.grahn@littvet.uu.se

H. Wahlström Henriksson et al. (Eds.), *Narratives of Motherhood and Mothering in Fiction and Life Writing*, Palgrave Macmillan Studies in Family and Intimate Life, https://doi.org/10.1007/978-3-031-17211-3_2

with both pro-life and pro-choice groups supporting each other globally (Morgan and Michaels 1999, 2). Indeed, the many women travelling abroad for the procedure convey the international scale of the issue. While I was working on "Tiger Bites," a Lucia Berlin short story about a 19-year-old crossing the Texas-Mexico border to terminate a pregnancy, abortion rights in the US were crumbling.[1] In September 2021, new Texas legislation made practically all abortion illegal in the state (Astor 2021). This was followed by the Supreme Court's overturning of *Roe v. Wade* in June 2022 (Liptak 2022).

We have yet to grasp the full impact of the Supreme Court ruling, even if reactions have been strong and immediate. One way of processing the events of the present and the memories of past experiences is through art and literature. Examining fictional stories of abortion can help us understand the cultural and political discourse concerning the subject. It can also give insight to the experiences of women regarding their reproductive health and possible options when it comes to their life decisions. As Heather Latimer writes: "fictional representations of reproduction offer a chance to examine reproductive politics outside cyclical frames concerned with rights and choices. [...] Fiction, like other forms of representation, responds to and reflects not only the culture in which it is produced but also that culture's ideological gaps" (Latimer 2013, 5).

In Anglophone literature, early examples of depictions of abortion include the British authors Jean Rhys' *Voyage in the Dark* (1934) and Aldous Huxley's *Eyeless in Gaza* (1934), which researchers have described as groundbreaking in their openness and lack of judgment (Minogue and Palmer 2006). In the case of Canadian author Margaret Atwood, well known for novels about women's oppression and resistance, *Surfacing* (1972) portrays an abortion which has primarily been discussed as reflective of problematic relations between Canada and the US, an interpretation that more recently has been criticized (Gault 2007). Previous research on how abortion is thematized in US literature suggests that it is a topic that is often avoided. Some have suggested that this is for fear of making the topic too complex and thereby unintentionally creating arguments for the pro-life movement (Bigman 2019).

---

[1] This chapter concentrates on an American literary text, and thus the cultural and historical context of that story, but abortion is illegal or difficult to access in many parts of the world. For a map over the current abortion laws of the world, see https://reproductiverights.org/maps/worlds-abortion-laws/

However, there are also authors from the US who do examine the subject. One of them is Lucia Berlin (1936–2004), who wrote most of her stories in the 1970s and 1980s but became well known and critically acclaimed with the posthumous short story collection *A Manual for Cleaning Women* (2015). The experiences of motherhood and mothering that Berlin conveys connect different times and places to each other, and show the relevance of storytelling across generations.

In this essay, I present a reading of Lucia Berlin's short story "Tiger Bites," one of the stories in *Manual...*, which follows the trajectory of a young woman crossing the American border to visit a Mexican abortion clinic. Lou is a 19-year-old mother who travels home to El Paso, Texas, with her small child to visit her kin over Christmas. Her husband has just left the family, and Lou is expecting their second child. At the train station her cousin Bella Lynn meets her and convinces her to travel across the border to Mexico to have an abortion. At the clinic, Lou regrets her decision and returns without going through with the procedure.

The analysis will center on how the subject of motherhood interconnects with concepts such as place, home, loneliness and agency that become apparent in the depiction of the abortion clinic. I argue that while not explicitly activist, the story is political in Jacques Rancière's sense as it "makes visible what was invisible, it makes audible as speaking beings those who were previously heard only as noisy animals" (Rancière 2011, 4). This interpretation of the political becomes especially relevant in the descriptions of the medical procedures, as they illuminate events that have previously been carried out in secret. In an issue of *London Review of Books* (July 2022) primarily focused on the overturning of *Roe v. Wade*, many authors made a similar point. Toril Moi writes:

> Silence is both the tool and the effect of repression. Silence ensures that the pregnant woman's fear and desperation will remain unheard, unheeded, unacknowledged. It ensures that women dying from botched backstreet abortions will be discreetly buried, not publicly mourned as victims of a cruel and inhumane policy (Moi 2022, 13).

By exploring the complexities surrounding motherhood, choice and independence, as well as bearing witness to the consequences of inaccessible abortions and reproductive healthcare, Berlin makes a case for empathy and solidarity with the women about whom she writes.

Lou is the first-person narrator, which makes the storytelling personal and moving, but also, obviously, unreliable. Lou is evasive and slightly sarcastic. As we will see, humor is used to defuse difficult topics and conversations, and I argue that Lou's relationship to family and motherhood affects the storytelling. It is worth noting that Lou is narrating from a double position of both mother and daughter. All mothers are certainly daughters, but Berlin makes it particularly evident, as Lou in her mind moves between her relationship with her mother and her relationship with her children and their future together. The point of view gives Lou narrative agency, as well as a possibility to express vulnerability both in her experiences at the abortion clinic and her feelings of abandonment by her own mother.

In the following sections, I begin by analyzing the visit to the abortion clinic itself, and the events taking place there. The next section addresses the mother figures in the story, examining the absence of "good" mothers and the potential for agency that their absence produces. The last section examines the places and homes that figure in the story, and how they connect to the maternal body.

## AT THE CLINIC

The heart of the short story is the visit to the Mexican abortion clinic. Lou goes back and forth between chosen and not-chosen motherhood, and is apparently uncertain about the abortion. It is Bella Lynn who convinces her to go to Mexico, by telling her how hard it will be to find work or another man while raising two children on her own. Learning about the pregnancy, she also reminds Lou about her parents: "Your ma will just kill herself all over again when she hears *this* news" (Berlin 2016, 73). As Lou and Bella Lynn drive across the border, and Lou gets picked up by a car and taken to a clinic outside of the city, the reader understands that she is in fact returning: Lou has spent time in Juárez as a child and speaks Spanish.

At the clinic, there are 20 other American women, some of them girls with their mothers. Here, the narrative becomes detailed and time slows down. The description of the women bears witness from a time before legal abortion: "Every one of them looked frightened, embarrassed, but most of all, intensely ashamed. That they had done something terrible. Shame. There appeared to be no bond of sympathy between any of them; my entrance was scarcely noticed" (Berlin 2016, 77). The nurse's brief and clinical description of the abortion gives the reader an insight to the procedure:

At five o'clock the doctor will come. You will have exam, catheter placed in utero. During the night cause contractions but sleeping medicine, you won't feel bad. No food, water after dinner. Early morning spontaneous abortion most usually. Six o'clock you go to operating room, go to sleep, get D and C. Wake up in your bed. We will give you ampicillin against infection, codeine for pain. At ten car will take you to Juárez or to El Paso Airport or bus (Berlin 2016, 77).

The nurse's curt language shows her level of English—we are reminded that we are outside of the US—but it also reflects the general atmosphere of the clinic. The woman showing Lou in is "so devoid of usual Mexican warmth and graciousness it felt like an insult" (Berlin 2016, 76). There are signals of preconceptions about Mexicans and their culture in Lou's words, and an expectation to be treated in a certain way. The portrayal of the Mexican doctor also emanates from presumptions about Latin American men, describing him as dark, handsome, and sexist—feeling up his patients and being condescending to them in Spanish. It is not until Lou speaks back to him in Spanish that he becomes respectful. Lou's girlhood memories of Juárez come to an abrupt end at the clinic where she instead is forced to take responsibility for herself and for others.

When Lou arrives at the clinic and sees the other women, she changes her mind about the abortion. Everyone in the room seems essentially alone: "The young girls perhaps most of all, for even though two of them were crying, their mothers also seemed distant from them, staring out into the room, isolated in their own shame and anger" (Berlin 2016, 78). This reminds Lou of her own situation: "Tears started to come to my eyes, because Joe was gone, because my mother wasn't there, ever" (Berlin 2016, 78). However, Lou's perspective changes:

I didn't want to have an abortion. I didn't need an abortion. The scenarios I imagined for all the other women in the room were all awful, painful stories, impossible situations. Rape, incest, all kinds of serious things. I could take care of this baby. We would be a family. It and Ben and me. A real family. Maybe I'm crazy. At least this is my own decision. Bella Lynn is always telling me what to do (Berlin 2016, 78).

With the last three sentences, the narrative changes into present tense, stressing the thought process: "Maybe I'm crazy. At least this is my own decision. Bella Lynn is always telling me what to do." Lou goes from being sad and abandoned by her mother to taking control over her life and her actions. She realizes she is a mother herself and that she can create "a real family."

The situation is at first devoid of sisterhood or care for each other. Everyone is alone, encapsulated in their own trauma. However, after changing her mind, Lou finds herself in-between positions of patient and caregiver. She must stay at the clinic overnight, and when the doctor realizes that she knows Spanish, she gets to help, translating and aiding the nurses. Particularly one of the young girls, Sally, is terrified and in need of soothing. Her mother is drunk and mentally absent, and watches as Lou and the doctor insert the long tube with the liquids to end the pregnancy. During the night, Lou wakes up and realizes the girl's bed is empty. She finds her bloody and unconscious on the bathroom floor. Berlin writes: "Blood was everywhere. She was hemorrhaging badly, tangled up in coils and coils of tubing like a berserk Laocoön. The tubing had clots of bloody matter sticking to it. It arched and buckled, slithering around her as if it were alive. She had a pulse but I couldn't rouse her" (Berlin 2016, 82).

Lou contacts the nurse who puts her to bed again and sedates her. When she wakes up in the morning, Sally and her mother are gone. The staff say that the girl is fine, but the reader is not reassured. Sally is likened to Laocoön, a name from Greek and Roman mythology with a long literary history. The mention of this mythical figure seems significant, in a story where literary references are rare. In one of the stories told about him, Laocoön is punished for breaking an oath of celibacy and having children, and thus the gods send giant snakes to kill him and his children (*Encyclopedia Britannica*, "Laocoön"). Other literary representations include that by Virgil in the *Aeneid*, where he is punished for warning the Trojans about the Greek wooden horse. Before the snake attack, Virgil describes Laocoön attacking the horse:

> He broke off then
> And rifled his big spear with all his might
> Against the horse's flank, the curve of belly.
> It stuck there trembling, and the rounded hull
> Reverberated groaning at the blow. (*Aeneid* II 71–75)

Laocoön, then, can be seen as both the attacked and the attacker. In the case of the wooden horse, its portrayal so close to that of a pregnant person, trying to destroy the enemy carried within is what kills the attacker. In both versions, pairing Sally with Laocoön means seeing Sally as punished—rightly or not—for defying higher powers. However, the description of Sally on the floor is, more than anything, a searing image of a child in pain. Lying there, surrounded by bloody tubes, she appears as a fetus or a newborn child. In a way, Sally becomes the fetus that is aborted instead of the one in Lou's uterus.

The detail and the precision of the portrayal of the abortion clinic give the scenes a strong sense of realism. This is also where Berlin is most empathic; in contrast to the rest of the short story, the shame and fear are not met with jokes or irony. Instead, the concern about Sally is real and piercing. However, when Lou leaves the clinic, Sally disappears from the story. Lou tells Bella Lynn about her experience, after which she concludes: "We Moynihans, though, we cry or get mad and then that's that" (Berlin 2016, 84). The girls go shopping and drinking, and after they leave the hotel there is no mention of the clinic or Sally. While being a central part of the short story, Sally and the abortion clinic nevertheless appear as isolated incidents. Since Lou does not have the abortion, it is almost as if she was never there. What has changed is the fact that Lou has made a decision on her own, not only because her husband and mother have abandoned her, but also because she has realized that she can create a family on her own. The abortion clinic has confronted her with her loneliness and consequently made her realize her own agency.

## DISTANT MOTHERS

While the story mainly centers on Lou's decision to continue her pregnancy and become a mother again, it also contains several other mother figures, who are all equally distant and evasive. Marilyn Francus has written about the "spectral mothers" in Western literary history, which, she writes:

> brings to the forefront the issue of haunting, which marks the ideological work of these maternal narratives: whether it is mothers who are haunted by absent children, or a preferred motherhood they cannot enact; or children who are haunted by an absent mother or a maternal ideal that their mothers fail to embody; or a society that is haunted by an ever-desired, ever-receding maternal ideal that domestic ideology cannot bring into being. The Western ideology of motherhood is aspirational, marked by hope, effort, loss, and desire (Francus 2017, 27).

Historically, Francus writes, normative and "good" mothers would not discuss their home life in public, which has meant that the few times that motherhood has been discussed or depicted, it has been the "bad" mothers who have been centered. The mothers in "Tiger Bites," and indeed in most of Berlin's writing, are failing the aspirational Western ideal of motherhood that Francus describes. I will now turn to how the absent and/or "bad" mothers of "Tiger Bites" create a space for Lou to grow into.

The three most important mothers in the story are those of Lou, Bella Lynn, and Sally, who all share similar traits: they are unsupportive and they are alcoholics. Sally's mother sits passively by her daughter's side, unable to care for her. Instead, it is Lou who has to explain the procedure to Sally and support her through it. Lou and Sally bond over their mothers' drinking:

> "Will your mama be alright?" I asked.
> "She'll be sick in the morning." Sally lifted the mattress. There was a half-pint of Jim Beam. "If I'm not here and you are, this is for her. She needs it so she don't be sick."
> "Yes. My mother drinks too," I said (Berlin 2016, 81).

Excessive drinking is a common characteristic for Berlin's mother figures. As Bella Lynn tells Lou: "your mama and my mama started drinking and fighting right off the bat. Mama went up on the garage roof and won't come down. Your mother slit her wrists. … She wrote a suicide note about how you had always ruined her life. Signed it Bloody Mary" (Berlin 2016, 70). Indeed, it might be said that lonely or hurt children are the true main characters of the story. "Tiger Bites" ends with Bella Lynn asking her father how she and Lou will cope, pregnant and left by their husbands. "Hope you two have knockout outfits for tomorrow's party," the father answers (Berlin 2016, 87). What is more, we never find out what happened to Sally, either before or after her visit to the clinic, although the doctor suspects that her father is responsible for her pregnancy. Bella Lynn, Lou, and Sally are all, in a sense, marked by their parents' abandonment.

Francus partly explains the Western narrative of the "bad" mother as a source for the more interesting story: "the telling of the 'bad' mother tale allows the author and the reader the pleasure of moral superiority: to expose the 'bad' mother, and to criticize and punish her for her 'bad' behaviors" (Francus 2017, 29). This is not, I would say, the case in "Tiger

Bites." The mothers are "bad" in the context of Western motherhood that we all recognize, but in the story they, like the women at the abortion clinic, are described matter-of-factly, without judgment.

Even though the overall feeling at the abortion clinic is a sense of shame, the narrative also has room for humor. The titular "tiger bites" allude to traumas that no one speaks about, that are met with jokes and money: "I used to think if a big old tiger bit off my hand and I went running up to my mother she'd just slap some money on the stump. Or make a joke ... 'What's that, the sound of one hand clapping?'" (Berlin 2016, 75). The one lonely clapping hand serves as a comical image of the severed family relations. Lou is abandoned by her mother, her husband, and the wider society, which does not offer her safe reproductive healthcare. Lou's dry, sometimes sad, sometimes funny, account of this situation reproduces her mother's joke.

In the introduction to the anthology *The Absent Mother in the Cultural Imagination* (2017), Berit Åström presents four explanations for the absent mothers of Western literature. The reasons mentioned are biographical, psychoanalytic, historical, or narratological (Åström 2017). Because of the auto-fictional nature of Berlin's writing, and the repeatedly distant and problematical mother-daughter relationships she portrays, the biographical explanation does have some weight in analyzing the distant mothers in "Tiger Bites." More interesting, though, is the explanation of the distant or dead mother as a narrative device. I do not claim that the mothers in "Tiger Bites" are portrayed as they are because of narratological convenience; on the contrary, they are very important for the construction and the content of the story. Although it might seem cynical to interpret the painful and problematic mother-daughter relationships simply as a way to drive the story forward, it is clear that the absent mothers leave a space for Lou to step into. Writing about mothers in Victorian novels, Natalie J. McKnight observes that an absent mother can instigate and motivate a character to act, as she "creates a vacuum that destabilizes the protagonists and therefore incites their development" (McKnight 1997, 18). I argue that this is the case in "Tiger Bites," too. While Lou is already a mother, her experience at the abortion clinic gives her opportunity to see herself as *the* mother figure, in place of her own mother and the other disappointing mothers in the story.

## PLACES, BODIES AND BORDERS

The issue of abortion is obviously linked to time and place, as legislation and cultural attitudes vary across geographies and historical time. It is also connected to wider political subjects; as Weingarten demonstrates, the American debate about abortion has been closely linked to eugenics and race politics (Weingarten 2014, 66). While race is not an explicit theme in Berlin's short story, the border between Mexico and the US is of great importance, and the dichotomy of home versus foreignness is highly relevant. Feminist scholars have made the connections between motherhood and nationalism for decades, and historically, the resistance against abortions has been connected to a fear of falling demographics (Yuval-Davis 1997, 26). The spatial aspects of Berlin's story, the idea of "home," and the crossings of geographical, political and bodily boundaries are therefore significant.

The story takes place sometime before the 1973 *Roe v. Wade* court case, which made abortion legal in the US. Therefore, Lou and the other women at the clinic have to go to Mexico. Coincidentally, her family home is in Texas, which was where the *Roe* case began, but also where, in 2021, all abortion was again essentially banned (Astor 2021). The hypocrisy and absurdity of the healthcare and judicial system is revealed in Bella Lynn's remark: "They can save your life and everything in Texas. They just can't do abortions" (Berlin 2016, 74). As *Roe v. Wade* was overturned in 2022, stories about people trying to leave the state to get access to abortions reappeared. In an article for *The New Yorker*, pharmacists in Juárez were interviewed about American women coming to buy misoprostol, an abortion inducing medication (Taladrid 2022). The risks involved in taking medicine without professional guidance, not to mention the risk of crossing the border for the many undocumented people now living in the area, makes this a highly dangerous solution. With modern possibilities of tracking people's movements, Texas lawmakers are even threatening to make it illegal to help someone travelling out-of-state for an abortion, which in turn could possibly create a system of control of any pregnant person, legally binding them to one place (Noor 2022). For a contemporary reader, the location therefore comes with a sense of foreboding, as a contextually transformative place. Depending on what decade you place Berlin's story in, the meaning of an unwanted or complicated pregnancy will change entirely. At the same time, the history of abortion along the Mexican border illuminates the intergenerational trauma surrounding the issue: the experiences of different generations of women are yet another blurred boundary.

In "Tiger Bites" various homes have been left and/or returned to. The home that Lou shared with her husband is gone, as he has left her to be an artist in Italy. Bella Lynn has a broken marriage behind her, too, and has just returned to her parents as her husband has gone to work at an oilrig. The money that Lou uses to pay at the clinic has been given to her by Bella Lynn, who in turn has received the money from her parents as an effort to console and distract her from the break-up with her husband. Within the wider theme of being a young woman creating a family, the story of Bella Lynn also serves a purpose of showing the importance of class and the arbitrariness of the law. As it turns out, not only abortion is illegal: "can you imagine, going down on your own lawful wedded husband is against the *law?*" (Berlin 2016, 72). The money, then, becomes both a symbol and material proof of the concerns of class and respectability that surround abortion, and indeed all sexual activities of women.

Conversely, the short story also depicts two homecomings. The girls are returning to the family ranch in El Paso to celebrate Christmas. The trip to Mexico is also a form of homecoming, since it turns out that Lou used to live there. The two homes, and their different atmospheres and associations, are juxtaposed in the story. Lou associates El Paso with "Jesus and Mary and the Bible and sin" (Berlin 2016, 69). As we will find out, her relationship with her family is not great. Her parents disapproved of her marriage, and the divorce is "the last straw" (Berlin 2016, 69). None of them will be at the family reunion, her father furious about the divorce and her mother in hospital after a suicide attempt. Lou seems cut off and distant from her immediate family. When they return home to the family to celebrate Christmas, the home is described as a strange and impersonal place: "The dining room table resembled the ads for smorgasbords on cruise ships" (Berlin 2016, 85). The people there are remote family members who "barely took their eyes from their plates or the game" as Lou enters (Berlin 2016, 85). Even so, she evidently feels a strong kinship with her family as she repeats how "us Moynihans" are.

Meanwhile, the trip to Mexico is more of a happy reunion. In the cab, Berlin writes: "I buzzed the window down and hung my head out, glad to be home" (Berlin 2016, 75). Aged 19, Lou is still a teenager. Yet returning home does not mean being cared for by her parents, and the older family members seem to be occupied with their own traumas and conflicts. Instead, it is in Mexico that Lou feels like a child: "The din and the smells of downtown Juárez were the same as when I was a little girl. I felt little and like I wanted to just wander around, but I waved for a cab" (Berlin 2016, 83). The hotel in Mexico is presented as more home-like than the ranch in Texas. As Bella Lynn says: "Hotels are so homey, I always hate to leave …" (Berlin 2016, 84).

Lou's relationship to the two places is not black and white. As is typical for Berlin, her protagonist's feelings about her homes and her family are ambiguous. The Spanish language serves as a good example of this. Lou speaks Spanish but does not immediately disclose this to other Spanish speakers. It is presented as more intimate than English: "She spoke a little English but I didn't speak any Spanish to her, or to any of them; it would have seemed too familiar a thing to do" (Berlin 2016, 77). Lou's bilingualism makes her a translator and mediator between the Mexican healthcare professionals and the American patients, which is just one of the ambiguous or in-between positions Lou takes in the story. Her movement between the US and Mexico, English and Spanish, patient and caregiver, mother and child is repeated throughout the story. It is when she arrives at the clinic, that things come to a head, and Lou has to make a choice.

I argue that this ambiguous relationship to the notions of home and family is replicated in Lou's almost-abortion. The maternal body serves as a home for the fetus, which can be seen either as an intruder or a welcome guest. Pregnancy and childbirth come with a crossing of bodily borders, as does abortion. As Adrienne Rich and others have argued, the institution of motherhood is revealed in maternal healthcare, in which women are subjected to patriarchal practices and attitudes (Rich 1976). The procedure of abortion is described as something that is done *to* the passive women: "the old woman started packing each woman's uterus with a ten-foot length of IV tubing, shoving it in, like stuffing a turkey" (Berlin 2016, 79). The description of the treatment of Sally is a particularly strong illustration of the invasiveness of the medical procedure, which, while undertaken in her own interest, possibly results in her death. It is important to note that the depiction of the abortion clinic and its staff is not about them being cruel. It is the situation itself, the unwanted pregnancies and the illegal abortions, which create the cruelty and the suffering.

Despite this violation of integrity, Lou's final decision is to keep the baby and make a home for it. Unlike Sally, who is a child, Lou has agency. She is free to make her own decision and has the power to protect herself from the intrusive doctor. In relation to the topics of homecoming and dysfunctional families, herself creating a family for her children seems, to her, like a way to break the cycle.

## CONCLUSION

This chapter has explored how abortion and motherhood feature in Lucia Berlin's short story "Tiger Bites," in which the feelings of loneliness, shame, desperation, and sadness are central. Even as the women are leaving the clinic, the oppressive atmosphere remains: "But the silence in the car was impenetrable, heavy with shame, with pain. Only the fear was gone" (Berlin 2016, 83). Abortion is not presented as a simple or obvious solution; the main character Lou decides not to do the procedure and comes home pregnant to have "a real family" (Berlin 2016, 78). One might interpret Lou's choice to continue her pregnancy as Berlin saying that abortion is only for the truly desperate. If possible—the devil's advocate interpretation might go—a woman will always choose to have a baby. The representation of abortion is not emancipatory or freeing; indeed, Lou's road to (imagined) independence goes through motherhood and creating a family of her own.

At the same time, the women in the story that do have abortions are depicted with empathy and solidarity. The complexity of the issue is reflected in the feelings surrounding the ideas of home and family, as motherhood is simultaneously the source of grief and loneliness, and the way out of those very feelings. Coming home to your family does not necessarily mean to feel cared for or safe, and the act of having an abortion means crossing borders and going to foreign places. However, the foreign place might be more familiar than the family home. Mexico represents Lou's childhood, while Texas, and the US, is characterized by the divided family: the alcoholic mother, the absent father and the runaway husband. In a fractured home, it is impossible to heal trauma.

The alcoholic, absent and cruel mothers of Sally, Lou and Bella Lynn merge into one dysfunctional mother figure, and their daughters are united in their handling of their mothers. The act of mothering consequently becomes fluid. Because of her pregnancy, Sally is a potential mother, while also a child. Lou herself is a young mother, who steps into a caring role when Sally needs to be calmed and helped through the abortion. There are no simple answers or clean-cut borders here; Lou's fluctuating position is key to understanding the ideas of both motherhood and homes.

To conclude, "Tiger Bites" is a story that portrays motherhood, as well as abortion, as a deeply complex subject connected to ideas of community and belonging. The breakthrough of Berlin's writing decades later goes to show that the issues and feelings depicted in the short story have been present for generations of women. Reading "Tiger Bites" in light of the recent overturning of *Roe v. Wade* makes it clear that storytelling is never linear, and that literary interpretation is closely linked to the society we live in. The unreliable nature of abortion laws, and indeed all rights of women and marginalized people, creates intergenerational trauma, which in Berlin's story is reflected in the dysfunctional mother-daughter relationships. This trauma, however, is not fatal. The isolation of the one hand clapping can be broken by caring for another. However, this is only possible when motherhood truly is a choice. As Berlin's portrayal of the abortion clinic illustrates, not having agency in deciding over your own body is the most isolating experience of all.

## References

Astor, Maggie. 2021. Here's What the Texas Abortion Law Says. *New York Times*, September 9, 2021. https://www.nytimes.com/article/abortion-law-texas.html

Åström, Berit. 2017. Introduction – Explaining and Exploring the Dead or Absent Mother. In *The Absent Mother in the Cultural Imagination. Missing, Presumed Dead*, ed. Berit Åström, 1–21. Basingstoke: Palgrave Macmillan.

Berlin, Lucia. 2016 [2015]. Tiger Bites. In *A Manual for Cleaning Women*, ed. Stephen Emerson, 69–87. London: Picador.

Bigman, Fran. 2019. Beginning with Abortion. *Los Angeles Review of Books*, November 7, 2019. https://lareviewofbooks.org/article/beginning-with-abortion/

*Encyclopedia Britannica*. Laocoön. https://www.britannica.com/topic/Laocoon-Greek-mythology

Francus, Marilyn. 2017. The Lady Vanishes: The Rise of the Spectral Mother. In *The Absent Mother in the Cultural Imagination. Missing, Presumed Dead*, ed. Berit Åström, 25–42. Basingstoke: Palgrave Macmillan.

Gault, Cinda. 2007. 'Not Even a Hospital': Abortion and Identity Tension in Margaret Atwood's *Surfacing*. *Atlantis: Critical Studies in Gender, Culture & Social Justice* 32 (1): 15–25.

Latimer, Heather. 2013. *Reproductive Acts: Sexual Politics in North American Fiction and Film*. Montréal: McGill-Queen's University Press.

Liptak, Adam. 2022. In 6-to-3 Ruling, Supreme Court Ends Nearly 50 Years of Abortion Rights. *New York Times*, June 24, 2022. https://www.nytimes.com/2022/06/24/us/roe-wade-overturned-supreme-court.html

McKnight, Natalie J. 1997. *Suffering Mothers in Mid-Victorian Novels*. Basingstoke: Macmillan.

Minogue, Sally, and Andrew Palmer. 2006. Confronting the Abject: Women and Dead Babies in Modern English Fiction. *Journal of Modern Literature* 29 (3): 103–125.

Moi, Toril. 2022. Prejudice Rules. LRB contributors on the overturning of *Roe v. Wade. London Review of Books*, July 22, 2022.

Morgan, Lynn M., and Meredith W. Michaels. 1999. *Fetal Subjects, Feminist Positions.* Philadelphia: University of Pennsylvania Press.

Noor, Poppy. 2022. Texas lawmakers test how far their threats against abortion can reach. *The Guardian*, July 24: 2022. https://www.theguardian.com/us-news/2022/jul/23/texas-republican-lawmakers-legal-threats-abortions.

Rancière, Jacques. 2011. *The Politics of Literature.* Translated by Julie Rose. Cambridge: Polity.

Rich, Adrienne. 1976. *Of Woman Born. Motherhood as Experience and Institution.* New York: W.W. Norton.

Taladrid, Stephania. 2022. A Texas Teen-Ager's Abortion Odyssey. The New Yorker, June 13, 2022. https://www.newyorker.com/magazine/2022/06/20/a-texas-teen-agers-abortion-odyssey

Virgil. 1990. *The Aeneid.* Translated by Robert Fitzgerald. New York: Vintage Books.

Weingarten, Karen. 2014. *Abortion in the American Imagination: Before Life and Choice, 1880–1940.* New Brunswick, New Jersey: Rutgers University Press.

Yuval-Davis, Nira. 1997. *Gender and Nation.* London: Sage.

# "their mothers, and their fathers, and everyone in between": Queering Motherhood in Trans Parent Memoirs by Jennifer Finney Boylan and Trystan Reese

*Elizabeth Podnieks*

## INTRODUCTION

In *Stuck in the Middle with You: A Memoir of Parenting in Three Genders*, Jennifer Finney Boylan (2013) muses, "There was a time once when motherhood and fatherhood were states as simple to define as *woman* and *man*. But as the meanings of *male* and *female* have shifted from something

This publication has received funding from the European Union's Horizon 2020 research and innovation programme under grant agreement No 952366, and from the Centre for Gender Research and the Department of Literature at Uppsala University.

E. Podnieks (✉)
Department of English, Toronto Metropolitan University, Ontario, Toronto, Canada
e-mail: lpodniek@ryerson.ca

H. Wahlström Henriksson et al. (Eds.), *Narratives of Motherhood and Mothering in Fiction and Life Writing*, Palgrave Macmillan Studies in Family and Intimate Life,
https://doi.org/10.1007/978-3-031-17211-3_3

33

firm and unwavering into something more versatile and inconstant, so too have the terms *mother* and *father* become more permeable and open-ended" (204). Urging us "to accept the wondrous scope of gender," she queries, "How many different kinds of fathers and mothers are there?" (205). In this chapter, I explore how Boylan's comments are addressed by Boylan herself, as well as by Trystan Reese (2021) in *How We Do Family: From Adoption to Trans Pregnancy, What We Learned About Love and LGBTQ Parenthood*. Boylan, a university professor then at Colby College in Maine[1] and best-selling author, reveals that she is a transgender woman who was a husband in a long-term marriage to Deirdre (Deedie) Finney Boylan, and father of their two children, Sean and (now) Zai.[2] Boylan writes from her position as a second mother and as the still-married "part-ner" of Deirdre Boylan (274). Reese, a social justice advocate, is a trans-gender man who not only adopted two children, Hailey and Lucas, with his husband, Biff Chaplow, but who also gave birth to their biological baby, Leo. In detailing their lives as transgender parents, Boylan and Reese illuminate how *mother* and *father* are concepts that are varied, mutable, and fluid, in narratives that are themselves structurally hybrid and innovative.

Both authors, married with children, operate within the framework of the white, middle-class nuclear family, advantaged by race, class, and sociocultural status. In my analysis herein, I argue that through narratives that conflate the conventional and the radical, Boylan and Reese normal-ize trans parenthood while queering normativity. Drawing on scholarship from queer, maternal, and life writing studies, and foregrounding the themes of transitioning, reproduction, and childrearing, I showcase how Boylan and Reese use their memoirs to document, probe, and celebrate what it means to queer motherhood. I contend that Boylan and Reese establish themselves as role models supporting and inspiring present and future generations of transgender parents. Pushing their private stories into the public realm, they make the personal both political and commu-nal; in so doing, they participate in and yet problematize the nuclear fam-ily, opening up vital spaces for new and inclusive notions of family.

---

[1] Boylan is now Professor and Anna Quindlen Writer in Residence at Barnard College of Columbia University ("About").

[2] Within the 2013 memoir, Boylan refers to her two children as sons. Boylan now notes on her website that she and "her wife, Deedie" are parents of "a son, Sean and a daughter, Zai" ("About"). In "Jennifer Finney Boylan: Love Prevails, Mostly" (*The New York Times*, June 16, 2019), Boylan explains, "Two years ago, in fact, my child sat next to me on the couch and told me she, too, was transgender." Within my chapter, I refer to Zai.

Before proceeding, I want to define some terminology, drawing on Susan Stryker's (2017) *Transgender History*. *Transgender* refers to "people who move away from the gender they were assigned at birth, people who cross over (*trans-*) the boundaries constructed by their culture to define and contain that gender" (1). Transgender has largely replaced *transsexuality* as "a one-way, one-time, medicalized transition across the gender binary" (38). *Cisgender* (*cis*, "on the same side as") means "nontransgender" (13). Relatedly, *queer*, "often used as a synonym for gay or lesbian," can be considered more of a political rather than a sexual orientation; *queer* also points to "the importance of transgender and gender-nonconforming practices for queer politics" (30–31).

Gender issues like these raise the question of pronouns. Gender-neutral pronouns can counter sexism and assumptions about one's gender identity. However, some trans people may prefer "appropriately gendered ones" in recognition of their hard-won attainment of their gender status (Stryker 2017, 24), as is the case with Boylan and Reese. Boylan (2013) tells us, "I'm transgender. I used to be a man, but I've been a woman for ten years now" (6–7), and describes being "someone who was a father" and is now "a mother" (225). In like manner, Reese (2021) acknowledges that despite being assigned female at birth, "I was clear about my gender identity"—"I was a boy who liked other boys, which made me gay" (3), and announces, "I came out as transgender at age nineteen" (2). As a parent, Reese is "Daddy" (Chaplow is "Dada"). As per their stated identities, I refer to Boylan and Reese respectively as she and he, mother and father. Below, I offer a close reading of their memoirs, which I first contextualize in theoretical, critical, and historical terms in the sections "Queering Mothers and Fathers" and "Trans Life Writing Traditions."

## QUEERING MOTHERS AND FATHERS

In considering what is at stake in merging the interests of queer and maternal theory, I look to *Queering Motherhood*, wherein editor Margaret F. Gibson (2014) states, "Queering makes the things we otherwise take for granted suddenly unpredictable, uncooperative, and unexpected" (1). In particular, she wonders what it would mean to queer motherhood (1–2). She attests that such an agenda has the potential to destabilize our previously held assumptions about "Reproduction, sexuality, culture, kinship, race, [and] embodiment," given their "intimate and expected connections to motherhood" (1–2). Insisting that queer perspectives be foregrounded in creative, sociocultural, and academic projects alike, Gibson calls on parents identifying as queer to articulate "stories and insights that might otherwise be drowned out by the din of cisnormative and heteronormative 'tradition'" (5), points that have particular relevance for my analysis of trans parent memoirs.

Gibson (2014) elaborates: "As a foundational social construct, 'motherhood' is invoked whenever we take parenting and reproduction seriously, regardless of whether or not the individuals involved are seen as, or believe themselves to be, 'mothers.' Even when we consider the practices and perspectives of queer fathers, transgender and transsexual parents, genderqueer parents, intersex parents, or even of queer people who did not ultimately become parents, we grapple with the institution of motherhood" (6). These issues resonate for Boylan, who became a mother only after being a father; and for Reese, a father who gave birth but was never a mother. On the one hand, Gibson posits that while maternal theory critiques the dominating ideologies of patriarchal institutional motherhood, it has not paid substantive attention to LGBTQ+ realities (10). On the other hand, "the classic canon of queer theory [...] has largely operated outside of the realm of the parental" (11). Like the contributors to her book, in my study of Boylan's and Reese's parenting memoirs I participate in a broader conversation that considers "what it might mean to re-think, re-shape, and re-establish notions and practices of motherhood from queer perspectives" (12).

Examining similar themes, Shelley M. Park (2020) details how queer theory "focuses on non-normative (i.e., non-procreative) forms of sexuality" concurrent with problematizing "the very gender binaries that seem to be pre-supposed by terms such as 'mother' and 'father'" (70). She highlights how some strands of feminism share with queer theory a rejection of patriarchal family structures predicated on women's domestication and procreation, and how these strands operate in tension with "another strand of feminism that celebrates the nurturing work of mothers and others and that views motherhood as empowering" (70). These tensions inform *Maternal Thinking* by Sara Ruddick (2002), who theorizes mothering as constitutive of a practice or work, which involves "preservative love, nurturance, and training" (17), and can therefore be performed by women and men alike (xii). Boylan (2013) refers to this treatise in her memoir: "According to Ruddick, men, too, are capable of 'mothering,'" yet Boylan confesses, "if someone had shared this theory with me when I was a father—and I identified as a feminist even then—it would surely have hurt my feelings. At the heart of this theory seems to be an assumption that caring for children is something women do. If you're a man and you're trying to nurture and protect your kids, it seems to me as if you're being called an honorary woman" (30). Boylan opposes, "There are lots of men who don't feel that expressing love makes them honorary women. One would think it makes them fathers" (30).

Boylan's comments speak to Reese, who identifies as a father. Damien Riggs (2013) helps us to appreciate Reese's paternity. Riggs states that depictions of trans men in social science literature and the media illuminate "a competition between transgender men's masculinity, and their undertaking of a role historically undertaken by people who identify as women (i.e., child bearing)" (62). Research reveals, however, that "pregnancy allowed transgender men to view their bodies as having a purpose" (68), and that "rather than making them feel *less* like men, instead vindicates for them that they *are* men precisely because they don't feel like a woman carrying a child" (69). With attention to Andrea Doucet's *Do Men Mother?* Riggs summarizes that Doucet's study of cisgendered men also applies to trans men, specifically, that neither can be considered mothers given how "tightly regulated" the term *mother* is "in relation to gender norms" (70). Riggs affirms that we need to distinguish birthing trans men "*as men,*" and "not default to norms for pregnancy defined historically by the experiences of women" (70). Ruddick's book was first published in 1989. Reassessing her arguments in the preface to the 1995 edition, Ruddick (2002) qualifies, "All mothering, whether done by men or women, depends on some particular woman's labor," that is, "still and only" by a woman's pregnant body (xiii). She also notes, "Even men who have been primarily responsible for mothering their children insist they are not mothers" (xiii). Ruddick thus denies birthing agency to trans men like Reese while supporting the findings of Riggs—that men self-identify "*as men*" (70).

Drawing on Ruddick's notion of maternal practice, Andrea O'Reilly (2021) theorizes what she calls a mother-focused or matricentric feminism. Such a feminism is required to counter the untenable patriarchal legitimation of so-called normative maternity, a discourse that constructs, promotes, and regulates "good mothers" as being women in nuclear families who are white, heterosexual, married, and economically dependent on their provider-husbands. In contrast, non-normative mothers—who are categorized as "de facto bad mothers"—may be "young, queer, single, racialized, trans, or nonbinary" (10–11). These "mother outlaws," as

O'Reilly calls them, "counter and correct as well as destabilize and disrupt normative motherhood" (11)—just as Boylan and Reese do in their memoirs.

O'Reilly (2021) takes up the contentious issue of terminology within matricentric feminism, in response to charges that "the term still excludes trans and non-binary folks" (12). However, the potential solution of employing the inclusive term *parent* might be "disingenuous if not dangerous because it deflects, disguises, and denies the very real and prevalent gendered oppressions of motherwork" (12). The challenge becomes "how do we include trans and nonbinary practices of parenting without excluding those of mothers" (29). Acknowledging these challenges, in my chapter I refer to parenting as a general, gender-inclusive practice, but I build my discussion specifically around shifting concepts of mother, mothering, and motherhood.[3] I take my cue from Gibson, for whom "Parenthood, fatherhood, family, and other social constructs may very well be simultaneously queered as we 'queer motherhood'" (6). I contextualize both Boylan's status as a former father and now mother and Reese's status as a birthing father within a framework that queers motherhood.

Scholars like Gibson (2014), Park (2020), and O'Reilly (2021) illuminate how trans parenting necessarily undermines normative patriarchal motherhood. Concurrently, Park, for example, introduces the term "homonormativity" (as coined by Lisa Duggan) to signal "the politics of respectability ushered in by (largely middle-class, white) gays and lesbians seeking state recognition of their relationships" (71). Here, "heteronormative forms of life (marriage, children, a home, a car, a pet, family vacations, wills, insurance, etc.)" indicate how "Homonormativity rewards lesbians and gays who mimic heteronormative standards," including those of parenting (71). In her study of twenty-first-century Swedish narratives, Jenny Björklund (2021) observes, "Queer readings of literature are typically focused on analyzing how heteronormativity is constructed and undermined in literary texts" (23). Yet, she cites scholarship by Ulrika Dahl and Rikke Andreassen positing that "non-heterosexual family formations have not really challenged traditional family models, especially the ideals of coupledom and the nuclear family" (6). Both Dahl and Andreassen ponder if queer kinship has in fact failed to be queer (6). These issues are taken up by Rachel Epstein (2009), who asks of queer families, "How do our families challenge, and how do they recreate, the conventional model

---

[3] By these terms, I mean respectively the person, the practice, and the institution.

of the heteronormative nuclear family and traditional notions of family, biology, blood, and kinship?" (22). She responds, "It is clear to me that we do both. We cannot parent outside of the cultural norms and discourses that shape our lives; and at the same time the existence of queer families, in all our diversity, cannot help but disrupt the heterosexual matrix" (22). Relatedly, Fiona Joy Green and May Friedman (2013) showcase stories that open "a lens on the messy and convoluted ways that querying parents approach parenting their children in gender aware and gender fluid ways" (2). Boylan and Reese likewise inscribe conventional and unconventional familial forms and practices as they normalize trans parenthood while queering normativity.

## TRANS LIFE WRITING TRADITIONS

The bourgeoning dialogue between queer and maternal scholars has led to unprecedented attention to trans parenthood. This attention has been made possible by, and is a reflection of, the increasing number of representations of trans mothers and fathers in twenty-first-century culture. Examples include the film *Transamerica*, Caitlyn Jenner's "Call me Caitlyn" *Vanity Fair* cover, the Amazon series *Transparent*, Sarah Savage's picture book *She's My Dad: A Story for Children Who Have a Transgender Parent or Relative*, Torrey Peters' novel *Detransition, Baby*, and online groups and resources like *transfertility.co* ("Everything you ever wanted to know about transgender fertility") and *milkjunkies.net* ("Breastfeeding and parenting from a transgender perspective"), founded respectively by Reese and by Trevor MacDonald. Perhaps the most groundbreaking intervention of trans parenthood within mainstream culture is the arrival of two new emojis. As announced by *Today's Parent* magazine on February 7, 2022, "One features a pregnant man and the other features a pregnant person, both created to recognize that not all people who get pregnant are women—some are trans men and non-binary folk" ("A pregnant man").

Trans subjectivity has especially been registered in trans autobiography and memoir.[4] Texts about transitioning began appearing in the early to mid-twentieth century, in tandem with medico-technological advancements involving hormone therapies and gender-affirming surgeries, and as a means by which trans individuals could assume authority over their

---

[4]Autobiography tends to focus on an entire life, whereas memoir treats a more limited period or thematic—as in parenthood.

stories, wresting control from the media which was intent on sensational-
izing them. Lili Elbe's *Man into Woman* (1933) is considered the first
book of its kind, [5] followed by Hedy Jo Star's *My Unique Change* (1965),
Christine Jorgensen's *Christine Jorgensen: A Personal Autobiography*
(1967), Jan Morris' *Conundrum* (1974), Renée Richards' *Second Serve*
(1983), Deirdre McCloskey's *Crossing: A Memoir* (1999), and Boylan's
*She's Not There: A Life in Two Genders* (2003), among many others.

It is only in the last fifteen years or so that memoirs foregrounding trans
parenthood have appeared. This genre was launched with Thomas Beatie's
*Labor of Love: The Story of One Man's Extraordinary Pregnancy* (2008b),
and further includes Boylan's *Stuck in the Middle with You* (2013), Trevor
MacDonald's *Where's the Mother? Stories from a Transgender Dad* (2016),
and Reese's *How We Do Family* (2021).[6] Just as trans life writing emerged
out of historical western traditions of autobiography, so trans parent memoirs are a crucial extension of largely heteronormative motherhood and
fatherhood memoirs appearing, respectively, in the late twentieth and early
twenty-first centuries.[7]

Life writing scholars highlight that many twentieth-century autobiographies about transitioning—those now deemed canonical—established
and adhere to a formulaic structure replete with clichéd themes. For
example, in *Second Skins*, Jay Prosser (1998) contends that "archetypal"
trans identity is shaped by "suffering and confusion; the epiphany of self-
discovery; corporeal and social transformation/conversion; and finally the
arrival 'home'—the reassignment" (101). Jonathan Ames (2005) traces a
similar narrative arc in his anthology of trans memoirs, *Sexual
Metamorphosis*. Plots like these are, to be sure, reductive.

In contrast, Chiara Pellegrini (2019) explores how twenty-first-century
trans life writers like Kate Bornstein and Juliet Jacques resist "transnormative" expectation, evidencing "growth and change and presenting challenges to normative gender beyond the supposed end of transition" (48).
In like manner, Boylan (2013) and Reese (2021) decenter transitioning as
they chronicle the ceaseless trials, responsibilities, and rewards attendant

---

[5] Ames suggests that Richard von Krafft-Ebing's 1886 *Psychopathia Sexualis* is "a pioneer-
ing collection of 237 case studies in sexual pathology," and constituting perhaps the earliest
first-person accounts of transgender identity (1).

[6] Bryant's *My Trans Parent: A User Guide for When Your Parent Transitions* is predicated
on first-person narratives of children of trans parents, generated through interviews, but also
includes several autobiographical pieces by trans parents, who were also interviewed.

[7] See O'Reilly (2010), Dymond and Willey (2013), and Podnieks (2016).

on parenthood. Relatedly, Sarah Ray Rondot (2016) finds the genre being advanced by contemporary trans autobiographers like Boylan as well as Alex Drummond.[8] According to Rondot, these writers "resituate themselves as active subjects rather than consumable objects, and envision gender as a fluid and diverse spectrum" (527). Consequently, they "reclaim agency by identifying in ways that depathologize trans* identity," and "expand what it means to narrate a trans* life by referencing yet resisting the traditional tropes associated with medical legitimation and dysphoria" (535). These points equally resonate with the strategies of Boylan in *Stuck in the Middle with You*, and Reese in *How We Do Family*, in terms of how they reference yet resist not only conventional medical narratives but also normative biological motherhood scripts.

### Stuck in the Middle with You

Boylan (2013) opens her narrative in the medias res of trans mothering, as she watches her teenage child, Zai, compete in a fencing tournament. She introduces herself to us accordingly: "I was a father for six years, a mother for ten, and for a time in between I was both, or neither, like some parental version of the schnoodle, or the cockapoo" (9). Emphasizing that she is "a parent who subverts a lot of expectations about gender" (9), she foregrounds that she is a queer mother who queers motherhood.

In a series of flashbacks early on, she outlines how she had identified as trans since childhood, but after falling in love with Deirdre, a social worker, in college, the two were married in 1988, with Boylan keeping her trans selfhood a secret. Describing the birth of their first child, Zai, Boylan (2013) addresses her readers: "Was I jealous, you ask, of Deedie's super-human powers, now that she was a mother?" and "did I feel left out, now that my love had experienced what may well be the defining moment in a woman's life?" (27). Boylan insists that she felt only lucky to have such a family, and then expands: "it wasn't maternity that I had yearned for. It was a sense of womanhood. Does that make me a hypocrite or a halfwit, to admit that I had dreamed of a woman's body, and a woman's life, and even the incredible gift of parenthood, without having any particular desire for pregnancy and menstrual cycles and breast-feeding?" (28).

---

[8] Rondot examines Boylan's second book of life writing, *I'm Looking Through You: Growing Up Haunted: A Memoir*, as well as Drummond's *Grrl Alex: A Personal Journey to a Transgender Identity*.

Boylan justifies that "surely a woman cannot be defined solely as a person who has borne children, or who has a menstrual cycle, or who has nursed a child" (28). In extricating mothering from biology and womanhood from maternity, Boylan creates space for her non-normative motherhood.

Zai was born in 1994; Sean, in 1996. By 1998, Boylan (2013) had "finally come out to [her] wife" (91), and by the summer of 2000 "was taking hormones and going through electrolysis" (107). Park (2020) notes, "When a person changes their public gender identity after a parental identity (as mother or father) has been previously established, this change will require negotiation within one's circles of intimacy" (66). Negotiating, "Either I stay with you, and lose the man I love most in the world, or I leave you, and I turn my back on the person I love right at the moment she most needs me," Deirdre Boylan chose to remain with Boylan (107). Deirdre Boylan further comments that the children were not significantly impacted because they were so young at the time of transitioning, and that they "continue to see Jenny as the parent that they've always loved" (268). When Boylan begins to transition, Zai observes, "We can't keep calling you 'Daddy'"—"If you're going to be a girl. It's too weird" (113). Zai proposes "Maddy"—"That's like, half Mommy, and half Daddy" (113), a term the family embraces as it participates in negotiating and queering motherhood.

Boylan (2013) generally refuses the transnormative narrative. She remarks: "I have written elsewhere [in *She's Not There*] about the details of the transition from male to female," and while she is "truly sorry to disappoint readers who are hoping to hear about all of those thrilling details one more time," she is "weary of stories of transsexuals always being stories about a trip to a hospital" (109). Boylan thus widens "what it means to narrate a trans* life by referencing yet resisting the traditional tropes associated with medical legitimation and dysphoria" (Rondot 2016, 535). Referring to surgery, Boylan contends, "That's not what being trans is all about. Being trans—and sustaining a family—is about everything that comes before that moment, and everything after. That's where the story lies" (109). Just as Rondot illuminates how innovative trans life writers "articulate a continuous subject rather than one split between pre- and post-transition" (527), and Pellegrini (2019) illuminates how they offer "challenges to normative gender beyond the supposed end of transition" (48), so Boylan's agenda is to focus on the more expansive "story"—here, that of "sustaining a family" as a parent.

On the one hand, Boylan (2013) presents her trans mothering as rebellious, replete with inevitable dangers. She wonders, what kind of adults "would my children become [...] having been raised by a father who became a woman?" (114). She confides, "I'd hear a voice in my heart demanding an answer to the same question my harshest critics had asked of me: What about the children?" (114). She "suspected that for the rest of their lives," she would be "waiting to see just how much damage" she had caused (163), but is relieved that to date her kids exhibit no "signs of trauma" (117). That said, Boylan appreciates their privileged status: "I'd heard stories first-hand from other trans people who, in nearly identical circumstances, had found only cruelty and rejection. Some had found violence" (165). Although Boylan herself did not experience such harm, she is candid about being transgender: "I knew better than anybody what a hard life it was" (179).

On the other hand, Boylan embraces homonormativity. She relays, "In the fall we picked apples. In the winter we skied and sat around the fireplace in our living room afterward, drinking hot chocolate. In summer we fished on Long Pond. [...]. Most of the time we forgot that there was anything extraordinary about our family. Were we really so strange?" (114). She remarks, "The thought of going through transition and coming out, and launching into some sort of subversive identity—well, let's just say it didn't appeal to me. I didn't want to be a revolutionary. A lot of the time, more than anything, I just wanted to be like everybody else" (20). This sentiment echoes Dahl and Andreassen's question about whether queer kinship is really all that queer (Björklund 2021, 6). Boylan admits, "I've been protested four or five times over the years. And about half of those times when I've been protested, it's been by transgender people," those "Disappointed that I'm not more radical" (275).

If Boylan (2013) is not as radical as some had hoped, she nonetheless underscores that the family as institution has long been subject to queering: "Only 7 percent of American households, according to the Population Reference Bureau, now consist of married couples with children in which only the father works. As it turns out, the biggest outlier in our culture is not same-sex couples, or transgender people, or adoptive parents, or single fathers, but the so-called traditional American family itself" (205–06). She surmises, "Every single family in the world is a nontraditional family" (206), thus queering all familial forms. Attending Zai's senior-year production of *Our Town*, Boylan describes the audience clapping loudly, while the student-actors "stood there, bowing and grinning, as they basked in the applause of their mothers, and their fathers, and everyone in between" (218). By dismantling what constitutes "traditional," Boylan democratizes kinship structures for conforming and non-conforming parents alike.

Boylan's (2013) queering of the family is paralleled by her queering of narrative form. Pellegrini (2019) highlights how contemporary trans life writers frustrate chronology with interludes and other interruptions to the narrative flow, effectively "pausing and denaturalizing" the main storyline (57). For example, the experiments of Bornstein and Jacques, who "mix their personal stories with gender theory and cultural analysis," draw attention to "the role of autobiographical narration in constructing identity in accordance with or in defiance of" transnormative models (46). Boylan is likewise innovative. Her text is organized around three main segments of autobiography, corresponding to her parental identities: "Daddy," "Maddy," and "Mommy." She inserts a "Time Out" section between each chapter, constituting a series of "Conversations" with multiple figures including authors, scholars, and activists like Richard Russo, Trey Ellis, Edward Albee, Barbara Spiegel, Dr. Christine McGinn, and Susan Minot, among others. They engage in discussion with Boylan about topics like gay parenting, trans conception, parenting an autistic child, parental mourning, adoption, African-American single fatherhood, parental ambivalence, and being childfree by choice. Boylan thus broadens the scope of the material and perspectives, offering a crucial intervention in her singular story as she moves from the personal to the communal. These "Time Out" breaks contribute to Boylan's "denaturalizing" not only of the chronology of memoir but also of normative motherhood *and* fatherhood.

In the afterword, Deirdre Boylan sums up her experiences with Boylan's transition: "I think the thing that is most surprising is perhaps how little has really changed, in the foundation of our relationship, in the foundation of our family and the way we operate" (Boylan 2013, 269). She thus contributes to the homonormative script of their lives while simultaneously queering normativity. Ultimately, as Boylan muses, happiness for herself obtains in the absence of gender: "freedom from gender means waking up in the morning and not having to think about it. I just kind of put my blue jeans on and go downstairs and feed the dogs. I don't really want to fight the gender fight every day. I don't have anything more to prove. And also, that there are as many ways of being trans as there are of being gay, or lesbian, or straight, or Irish, or anything else" (276).

Although Boylan has nothing "more to prove," with her memoir she proves that there are "many ways" of being a mother.

## How We Do Family

Reese (2021) foregrounds fatherhood in his memoir's first line: "Becoming a parent after only a year of dating was never the plan" (1). Living in Hollywood, and serving at the National LGBTQ Task Force as a senior organizer, Reese and his partner, Biff Chaplow, a social worker, "had celebrated our first anniversary as boyfriends and had just moved in together" when they were propelled into parenting (1). In 2011, Hailey and Lucas, Chaplow's niece and nephew, were at risk of being removed from their maternal home by Children's Protection Services, and so Chaplow and Reese took in the toddlers. While relaying this backstory, Reese introduces himself as having transitioned via hormone therapy as a young man. Refusing the transnormative narrative that builds toward transition, Reese gets these details out of the way so that he can privilege the story of his fathering.

This paternal narrative is, in many ways, homonormative. Reese and Chaplow formalized their nuclear family by legally adopting the children, after getting married in the summer of 2012.[9] The storyline of adoption is, however, only part of their parenting journey. The memoir shifts to a concentration on how Reese queers motherhood when he becomes a birthing father. Early in his relationship with Chaplow, Reese (2021) "had occasional dreams of a baby. She had dark, liquid eyes and long eyelashes, and when I saw her in these dreams, I felt the deepest longing I had ever experienced" (15). As the adoption becomes settled, Reese "again felt the pull of a baby" (93). Where Rondot (2016) argues that subversive trans memoirists advance the genre by "referencing yet resisting the traditional tropes associated with medical legitimation" (535), Reese adapts these strategies for his narrative of conception, pregnancy, and parturition.

For instance, Reese (2021) elucidates of his transition: "My ovulatory and menstrual processes were put on hold by the hormone shifts" and he was wrongly informed that testosterone would render him infertile (4). Years later, after much research, he learns that trans pregnancy is in fact

---

[9] Reese qualifies that gay marriage was not legal at the time; "It was really just the ceremony and party we were interested in" (57). Gay marriage became legal across the U.S. on June 26, 2015.

feasible. A trans friend recommends a fertility clinic: "He said they'd had a good experience at the Providence Maternal Care Clinic. I knew that most trans guys would bristle at the name ('maternal' is quite the gendered word, after all) but figured I couldn't be picky, or I might end up with no medical support at all" (99). Here, Reese must negotiate his needs for health care with a system that regards gestation as the sole province of women. Reese stops taking hormones, describing how his masculinization (facial hair and lower voice) due to transitioning would remain largely unchanged, but "a menstrual cycle and rapid mood swings were about to begin" (100). His path to becoming pregnant is therefore one of queering the medical establishment concomitant with queering the maternal body.

After an initial miscarriage, Reese again becomes pregnant (via "scheduled sex" with Chaplow (Reese 2021, 131)). He relays that "Hailey and Lucas both recognized that this would be a unique situation in their school community. None of their school friends' parents were transgender; there weren't any other gay dads at their school either" (138). He contemplates how "So many of the trans men I'd connected with online had shared stories of their kids being tormented by peers and even school staff when stories of their pregnancies had surfaced" (138–39), and he soon has to contend with Hailey being accused of lying by classmates, whose parents told them men can't have babies. Reese becomes driven to publicize their personal story. He thinks of "Laverne Cox, Janet Mock, Carmen Carrera … all of these amazing trans women of color, working tirelessly to push the culture forward by telling their stories and putting themselves out there again and again" (142). He determines to use "the 'hook' of a pregnant man to start a larger conversation about trans rights and families" (143–44).

Reese (2021) reaches out to the podcast *The Longest Shortest Time* to announce his pregnancy, gaining recognition as "the pregnant man" (144). According to Park (2020), "While transwomen have captured the public imagination as they become mothers to the children whom they previously fathered, transmen—such as Thomas Beatie who created a media sensation in 2008—have captured public attention in their role as birthgiving fathers" (66).[10] Indeed, Boylan (2013) recounts how, as a

---

[10] Ryan emphasizes that Beatie "was not the first trans man to become pregnant and he was certainly not the first trans man to be a father. Although medical advancements that allow for physical transition are relatively new, trans-identified people have always raised children" (140).

trans woman, she had "written a best-selling book [*She's Not There*], been a guest of Oprah Winfrey, even been imitated on *Saturday Night Live* by Will Forte" (9). Reese follows the cultural narrative of Beatie, who after transitioning gave birth to three children, in 2008, 2009, and 2010. On March 14, 2008, Beatie was featured on *Advocate.com* in the story "Labor of Love" with the caption, "Is society ready for this pregnant husband?" *People* magazine's July 3, 2008, issue then announced, "The Pregnant Man Gives Birth" (Beatie 2008a). That same year, Beatie published his memoir *Labor of Love*, the first trans memoir dedicated to the topic of parenthood and an obvious precursor to Reese's text.

Reese (2021) becomes, like Beatie and Boylan, a media sensation and is barraged by transphobia, "receiving hundreds of messages on social media every single day, telling me that I was going to give birth to a monster," and that "my body is disgusting" (145). Alisa Grigorovich (2014) posits that "Beatie's male identity is discredited through reference to his reproductive organs and his decision to become pregnant" (85). Moreover, "male pregnancy and the idea that one can be male and have a vagina disrupts the very contours of what is thought to be a (gendered) body, generating a repulsion of it" (89), reactions encountered by Reese. However, while Reese chronicles how the (cis-) public regards his pregnant body as "disgusting," by offering us his narrative on his own terms he claims authority and control over his image and recuperates legitimacy for the queer body.

We can see how he negotiates tensions like these as he documents how he progressively experiences pregnancy as physical distress. He is relieved to learn that the pain he senses is due to his very large fetus causing his ribs to separate: "It was nice to know that I hadn't been a weak man who couldn't handle the usual tortures of pregnancy. I had been a normal man who couldn't handle the particular torture of growing a baby that was too big for his body" (Reese 2021, 167-68). Reese invokes Riggs' (2013) research that pregnancy for trans men, "rather than making them feel *less* like men, instead vindicates for them that they *are* men precisely because they don't feel like a woman carrying a child" (69). As "a normal man" (Reese 2021, 168), Reese queers motherhood as he normalizes pregnancy from a male perspective.

Although Reese faced prejudice in the media, he was frequently treated with respect by the medical profession. For example, discussing his pending Caesarian delivery, his doctor informs Reese that he can choose to have a horizontal or vertical incision. While the former is "indicative of a

C-section," the latter could suggest numerous types of surgery; the doctor states, "I was simply considering that a vertical scar might be more affirming of your gender" (Reese 2021, 165–66). Reese is "blown away by this physician's attention to my gender identity" (166). Here, Reese counters what Paisley Currah (2008) finds to be the "larger story of discrimination in the health care industry" toward trans men like Beatie, as "ob-gyn offices or maternity wards" register a "stupefied resistance to bodies that confound gender expectations" (331). Grigorovich (2014) believes that, negativity notwithstanding, Beatie's story has "increased the visibility of transgender families in the mainstream" and led to positive "social change and activism" (93). To be sure, chronicling his own story, Reese highlights how ongoing trans advocacy and education have contributed to a medical queering of motherhood. That said, upon giving birth, "Hundreds of strangers on the internet asked me if I was going to breastfeed; so did journalists live on TV; so did every medical professional I encountered at every prenatal checkup I attended. I wanted to scream it from the mountaintops: STOP ASKING ABOUT MY BREASTS!!!" (181). He tells us, "I would not be bodyfeeding Leo" (180) because "I didn't want to use my body in that way" (182). While Riggs (2013) states that "pregnancy allowed transgender men to view their bodies as having a purpose" (68), Reese makes it clear that trans men, as much as women, have the right at all times to *choose* what those purposes will be. In claiming autonomy over how he feeds his child, Reese queers the normative scripts that seek to control and judge the reproductive body.

This medical queering is echoed in Reese's narrative structure, which is, like Boylan's, fragmented. Each of the nine chapter titles begin with "How," as in "How We Do Pregnancy" and "How We Do Parenting." The chronological sequence is interrupted by numerous interludes entitled "Notes from Life in Our Family," wherein Reese offers commentary on and practical information about issues discussed in the chapters, thereby "pausing and denaturalizing" the autobiography proper (Pellegrini 2019, 57). At the end of his narrative, Reese (2021) asks Hailey, "Do you ever wish you were in a different family? A more normal one?" She replies: "Never in a million, gajillion years" (193). Reese ponders, "'a gajillion' might be the exact right way to think about our family. Not in a gajillion years has there been a family like us, nor will there be in another gajillion. And that's true for every family that has ever been. Each is exquisitely unique and painstakingly ordinary" (194). Reese queers not only the transnormative plot but also normative constructions of family.

## CONCLUSION

Gibson (2014) praises the contributors to her essay collection for the ways they have "considered what it might mean to re-think, re-shape, and re-establish notions and practices of motherhood from queer perspectives" (12), as do Boylan and Reese in their memoirs. Boylan and Reese participate in what Park (2020) calls the "denaturalization" of motherhood (73); Park asserts that there is "no 'natural' way of becoming a mother, and no 'natural' body that a mother has," the former claim proven by Boylan, the latter by Reese (74). Likewise, with gratitude toward her collaborators, Epstein (2009) reflects, "We need to turn away from romanticized depictions of our families that deny our pains and challenges and complexities and move toward deeper, fuller accounts of our families. When I read the pieces in this book I am moved by the risks the authors take to speak openly about their experiences of queer parenting" (30). As evidenced in my chapter, Boylan and Reese take similar risks, ones that clearly yield rewards.

We can appreciate these optimistic outcomes through Riggs et al. (2021), who maintain that the study of trans parenting helps us to recognize not only "the agency enacted by trans parents but also to understand the positive experiences of parenting that trans people have" (812). Such is the overarching position waged by Boylan and Reese. Boylan (2013) contends, "I think I'm a loving person, and that I bring that to people. And that our family is better for having me around" (280). Reese (2021) describes Hailey and Lucas as constituting "the center" of his and Chaplow's world (79), and that being a father to Leo "was the only thing" he, Reese, has "ever been perfect at" (184). Reese further attests, "I am rebuilding the world around me with love" (188). Nurturing affirmations like these support Epstein's (2009) observation that "Recent years have seen an upsurge of trans activism and visibility, including an insistence on the right to parent" (20). As we have seen, Boylan and Reese use their memoirs to these urgent ends.

Rondot (2016) finds that for trans authors, autobiography serves as a site of rebellion and subversion, but such potential may be reserved only for people privileged as "white, middle-class, partnered, and able-bodied" (547). Park (2020) insists that studies of queer motherhood must transcend markers of mainstream status, especially via representations moving beyond the Global North (73). Jan E. Estrellado and Alanna Aiko Moore (2021) signal new directions in their interventional essay "Towards a

Queer and Trans Model for Families of Colour." Parents of two children, they introduce themselves accordingly: "Alanna is a mixed-race Asian queer femme (she/her/hers) married to Jan, a Pilipinx, queer, transmasculine, and non-binary person (who responds to all pronouns)" (137). Testifying from their personal perspectives that they "have limited access to a diversity of family models" (146), they assert: "Our family, who are in many ways just trying to exist the way most families do, offers one example of the added complexities related to feminism, race, queerness, and transness" (151).

Estrellado and Moore (2021) help us to appreciate how the field of trans life writing—radically advanced by Boylan (2013) and Reese (2021), both white and middle class—must continue to push forward by encouraging more diverse trans populations to tell their stories, and that these populations must be ensured access to resources enabling the production and publication of their narratives. Reese is eager to facilitate such developments. His appendix, "How We Do Activism," elucidates his and Chaplow's "lifelong commitment to anti-racism, and [their] inherited beliefs around justice" (195). Similarly, at the back of her text, Boylan provides a list of resources for and about trans families. Gibson (2014) observes that many of the recent books "about queer pregnancy, adoption, and parenting" have "crossed genre divides between academic, activist, literary, how-to, and humour writing" (5). Through their resources and their hybrid structures of storytelling, Boylan and Reese punctuate their personal narratives with ongoing attention to communal perspectives and calls for social justice.

Evan Vipond (2019)—like Rondot (2016) and Park (2020)—argues that the cultural intelligibility of memoirs by canonical authors like Jorgensen and Morris is predicated on their "proximity to whiteness" (21) and that such texts are "marketed to the general (read: cisgender) public" (20). Boylan and Reese, while writing through their white privilege, aim to disseminate their stories and attendant calls for action to a broad audience. They consistently address their readers as "you," employing the pronoun at times to distinguish, at other times to conflate, cisgender and trans perspectives. For instance, following her gender affirmation surgery, Boylan reports, "I was a forty-four-year-old woman who'd never had sex with a man," adding "I was curious about men, though. Wouldn't you be?" (181). In another reference to her surgery, she provides a list of resources "For the curious—as well as to serve as a guide for others with the same condition" (109). Reese similarly speaks to those like himself—"If you're a transgender person" (147)—while concurrently instructing a cis-audience: "Listen to the stories you hear from trans people" (197). Boylan's and Reese's fluid invocations to "you" bring their cis- and trans-readers together in a community of intersecting interests and values, and produce their own iterations of what Vipond calls "counternarratives that speak back" (21) to mainstream assumptions that the general reader is necessarily, or only, cisgender.

Boylan's (2013) and Reese's (2021) memoirs are part of what Stryker (2017) describes as "a rapidly growing body of fiction and nonfiction literature, academic writing, documentary films, television shows, movies, blogs, YouTube channels, and other forms of DIY cultural production by and about trans people that places us in cultural and historical context and imagines us as part of communities and social movements" (2). Rondot (2016) emphasizes that trans life writings can be "liberatory because they contribute to a multivocal conversation about gender, expand cultural knowledge, and offer new and different ways to narrate and understand diverse trans* lives" (547). Boylan and Reese are in the vanguard as they chronicle their trans mothering and fathering, respectively. My analysis of *Stuck in the Middle with You* and *How We Do Family* signals how queer, motherhood, and life writing studies gain increasing relevance and vitality when their praxes intersect and expand in relation to each other. Boylan's and Reese's narratives exemplify possibilities for familial restructuring that critique, resist, and transcend cisgendered patterns and assumptions about embodiment, reproduction, and caregiving. While the memoirs embrace homonormativity, they concurrently stage dramatic interventions in heteronormative paradigms, and in so doing, they normalize trans parenthood while queering motherhood.

## REFERENCES

A pregnant man emoji is here and it's about damn time. *todaysparent.com*. February 7, 2022.

Ames, Jonathan. 2005. Introduction. In *Sexual Metamorphosis: An Anthology of Transsexual Memoirs*, ed. Jonathan Ames, ix–xvi. New York: Vintage Books.

Beatie, Thomas. 2008a. Labor of Love. *Advocate.com*, March 14, https://www.advocate.com/news/2008/03/14/labor-love.

———. 2008b. *Labor of Love: The Story of One Man's Extraordinary Pregnancy*. Berkeley: Seal Press.

Björklund, Jenny. 2021. *Maternal Abandonment and Queer Resistance in Twenty-First-Century Swedish Literature*. Gewerbestrasse: Springer Nature Switzerland. https://doi.org/10.1007/978-3-030-72892-2.

Bornstein, Kate. 2016. *Gender Outlaw: On Men, Women, and the Rest of Us*. New York: Vintage.

Boylan, Jennifer Finney. 2022. About. https://jenniferboylan.net/about/.

———. 2008. *I'm Looking Through You: Growing Up Haunted: A Memoir*, 2008. New York: Broadway.

———. 2019. Jennifer Finney Boylan: Love Prevails, Mostly. *The New York Times*. June 16. https://www.nytimes.com/2019/06/16/us/jennifer-boylan-transgender-woman.html.

———. 2003. *She's Not There: A Life in Two Genders*. New York: Broadway Books.

———. 2013. *Stuck in the Middle With You: A Memoir of Parenting in Three Genders*. New York: Broadway Books.

Bryant, Heather. 2020. *My Trans Parent: A User Guide for When Your Parent Transitions*. London: Jessica Kingsley Publishers.

Call me Caitlyn. 2015. June 25, *Vanity Fair*.

Currah, Paisley. 2008. Expecting Bodies: The Pregnant Man and Transgender Exclusion from the Employment Non-Discrimination Act. *WSQ: Women's Studies Quarterly* 36 (3 & 4 (Fall/Winter)): 330–336. https://doi.org/10.1353/wsq.0.0101.

Doucet, Andrea. 2006. *Do Men Mother?: Fathering, Care, and Domestic Responsibility*, 2006. Toronto: University of Toronto.

Drummond, Alex. 2012. *Grrl Alex: A Personal Journey to a Transgender Identity*. Worthing: Bramley.

Duggan, Lisa. 2004. *The Twilight of Equality? Neoliberalism, Cultural Politics, and the Attack on Democracy*. Boston: Beacon Press.

Dymond, Justine, and Nicole Willey, eds. 2013. *Motherhood Memoirs: Mothers Creating/Writing Lives*. Toronto: Demeter Press.

Elbe, Lili. 1933. *Man Into Woman*, edited by Niels Hoyer, translated by H. J. Stenning, introduced by Norman Haire. London: Jarrold Publishers.

Epstein, Rachel, ed. 2009. Introduction. In *Who's Your Daddy? And Other Writings on Queer Parenting*, ed. Rachel Epstein, 13–32. Toronto: Sumach Press.

Estrellado, Jan E., and Alanna Aiko Moore. 2021. Towards a Queer and Trans Model for Families of Colour: Intersections of Feminism, Race, Queerness, and Gender Identity. In *The Liminal Chrysalis: Imagining Reproduction and Parenting Futures Beyond the Binary*, ed. Kori Doty and A.J. Lowik, 137–152. Toronto: Demeter Press. Kindle Edition.

Gibson, Margaret F. 2014. Introduction: Queering Motherhood in Narrative, Theory, and the Everyday. In *Queering Motherhood: Narrative and Theoretical Perspectives*, ed. Margaret F. Gibson, 1–23. Toronto: Demeter Press.

Green, Fiona Joy, and May Friedman. 2013. Introduction. In *Chasing Rainbows: Exploring Gender Fluid Parenting Practices*, ed. Fiona Joy Green and May Friedman, 1–19. Toronto: Demeter Press.

Grigorovich, Alisa. 2014. 'Pregnant with Meaning': An Analysis of Online Media Response to Thomas Beatie and his Pregnancy. In *Queering Motherhood: Narrative and Theoretical Perspectives*, ed. Margaret F. Gibson, 81–96. Toronto: Demeter Press.

Jacques, Juliet. 2015. *Trans: A Memoir*. London: Verso.

Jorgensen, Christine. 1967. *Christine Jorgensen: A Personal Autobiography*. New York: Paul S. Eriksson, Inc.

MacDonald, Trevor. 2016. *Where's the Mother? Stories from a Transgender Dad*. Winnipeg: Trans Canada Press.

McCloskey, Deirdre N. 1999. *Crossing: A Memoir*. Chicago: University of Chicago Press.

Morris, Jan. 2002. *Conundrum*. New York: New York Review of Books.

O'Reilly, Andrea. 2021. *Matricentric Feminism: Theory, Activism, Practice*. Toronto: Demeter Press.

———. 2010. The Motherhood Memoir and the 'New Momism': Biting the Hand That Feeds You. In *Textual Mothers/Maternal Texts: Motherhood in Contemporary Women's Literatures*, ed. Elizabeth Podnieks and Andrea O'Reilly, 203–213. Waterloo: Wilfrid Laurier University Press.

Park, Shelley M. 2020. Queering and Querying Motherhood. In *The Routledge Companion to Motherhood*, ed. Lynn O'Brien Hallstein, Andrea O'Reilly, and Melinda Vandenbeld Giles, 63–76. Abingdon: Routledge.

Pellegrini, Chiara. 2019. Posttranssexual Temporalities: Negotiating Canonical Memoir Narratives in Kate Bornstein's *Gender Outlaw* and Juliet Jacques's *Trans*. *a/b: Auto/Biography Studies* 34 (1): 45–65. https://doi.org/10.108 0/08989575.2019.1542820.

Peters, Torry. 2021. *Detransition, Baby*. New York: One World.

Podnieks, Elizabeth. 2016. 'Daddy Time All the Time': Representations of Involved Fatherhood in Contemporary Dadoirs. In *Pops in Pop Culture: Fatherhood, Masculinity, and the New Man*, ed. Elizabeth Podnieks, 67–86. New York: Palgrave Macmillan.

Prosser, Jay. 1998. *Second Skins: The Body Narratives of Transsexuality*. New York: Columbia University Press. Kindle.

Reese, Trystan. 2021. *How We Do Family: From Adoption to Trans Pregnancy, What We Learned About Love and LGBTQ Parenthood*. New York: The Experiment.

Richards, Renée. 1983. *Second Serve: The Renée Richards Story*. New York: Stein and Day.

Riggs, Damien W. 2013. Transgender Men's Self-Representations of Bearing Children Post-Transition. In *Chasing Rainbows: Exploring Gender Fluid*

*Parenting Practices*, ed. Fiona Joy Green and May Friedman, 62–71. Toronto: Demeter Press.

Riggs, Damien W., Sally Hines, Ruth Pearce, Carla A. Pfeffer, and Francis Ray White. 2021. Trans Parenting. In *Maternal Theory: Essential Readings*, ed. Andrea O'Reilly, 807–815. Toronto: Demeter Press.

Rondot, Sarah Ray. 2016. 'Bear Witness' and 'Build Legacies': Twentieth and Twenty-First-Century Trans* Autobiography. *a/b: Auto/Biography Studies* 31 (3): 527–551. https://doi.org/10.1080/08989575.2016.1183339.

Ruddick, Sara. 2002. *Maternal Thinking: Toward a Politics of Peace*. Boston: Beacon Press.

Ryan, Maura. 2009. Beyond Thomas Beatie: Trans Men and the New Parenthood. In *Who's Your Daddy? And Other Writings on Queer Parenting*, ed. Rachel Epstein, 139–150. Toronto: Sumach Press.

Savage, Sarah. 2020. *She's My Dad: A Story for Children Who Have a Transgender Parent or Relative*. London: Jessica Kingsley Publishers.

Star, Hedy Jo. 1965. *My Unique Change*. Chicago: Novel Books.

Stryker, Susan. 2017. *Transgender History: The Roots of Today's Revolution*. New York: Seal Press.

The Pregnant Man Gives Birth. 2008. July 3, *People Magazine*. https://people.com/parents/the-pregnant-man-gives-birth/.

*Transparent*. 2014–2017. Amazon Prime Video.

Tucker, Duncan, dir. 2005. *Transamerica*. Belladonna Productions.

Vipond, Evan. 2019. Becoming Culturally (Un)intelligible: Exploring the Terrain of Trans Life Writing. *a/b: Auto/Biography Studies* 34 (1): 19–43. https://doi.org/10.1080/08989575.2019.1542813.

# Struggling to Become a Mother: Literary Representations of Involuntary Childlessness

## *Jenny Björklund*

In Sweden the welfare state provides mothers with a high degree of support and flexibility, and gender equality and progressive family politics are crucial to the nation's self-image. The welfare state has also encouraged its citizens to reproduce through various pronatalist measures, such as paid parental leave, state-subsidized childcare, and monthly cash benefits for parents. Compared to other European countries, Southern European countries in particular, birth rates in Sweden and the other Nordic countries are relatively high (see, for instance, Björnberg 2016, 509–10; Esping-Andersen 2016). The number of Swedish women who never have children is not high from a European perspective (13.5%), but it still

This publication has received funding from the European Union's Horizon 2020 research and innovation programme under grant agreement No 952366, and from the Centre for Gender Research and the Department of Literature at Uppsala University.

J. Björklund (✉)
Centre for Gender Research, Uppsala University, Uppsala, Sweden
e-mail: jenny.bjorklund@gender.uu.se

H. Wahlström Henriksson et al. (Eds.), *Narratives of Motherhood and Mothering in Fiction and Life Writing*, Palgrave Macmillan Studies in Family and Intimate Life,
https://doi.org/10.1007/978-3-031-17211-3_4

55

means that almost one out of seven Swedish women are childless (Statistics Sweden 2020).[1]

As motherhood is still at the core of constructions of femininity, women who do not have children come across as unintelligible and are often represented in negative ways. In a study of cinematic representations of childlessness, Cristina Archetti (2019) shows how these portrayals of childless women are highly negative, regardless of the reasons they do not have children: "the childless tend to die, either by suicide or killed by others; if they do not die, they acquire a child against all expectations; only men and female (super) heroes can overcome the trauma of infertility; and childlessness by circumstance practically does not exist" (182; see also de Boer et al. 2019; Graham and Rich 2014). Cultural representations of women who try to have children but fail are rare, as media tends to give privilege to stories with happy endings. Rebecca Feasey (2019), who studies mainstream media representations of infertility and non-normative family building, highlights the discrepancy between the miracle-baby-in-the-end stories in the media and the harsh medical reality where fertility treatments fail more often than they succeed. She is particularly wary of this situation, as she points out that most people get their information about infertility from the media rather than medical literature.

This chapter focuses on three twenty-first-century Swedish novels that give slightly different images of women who struggle with infertility. In contrast with the cinematic representations in Archetti's study and the media representations in Feasey's, the women are not represented in negative ways, and the novels do not end with babies or even pregnancies. In this chapter I analyze literary representations of involuntary childlessness and the women at the center of these narratives, focusing in particular on how non-motherhood is positioned in relation to femininity and (hetero) normativity. I also situate these representations in their national context and analyze how they relate to Swedish-branded values like gender equality and progressive family politics.

I have selected three novels where the struggle to have children takes center stage and with female protagonists who are either first-person narrators or focalized by a third-person limited narrative: Pernilla Glaser's *40*

---

[1] All of these women are not involuntarily childless; according to the Public Health Agency of Sweden, 5% of the population do not want children (Folkhälsomyndigheten 2019). Furthermore, these statistics do not include women who have become mothers without giving birth, such as some mothers in same-sex relationships.

*minus* (2010; 40 Below), Martina Haag's *Glada hälsningar från Missångerträsk: En vintersaga* (2011; Happy Greetings from Missångerträsk: A Winter's Tale), and Tove Folkesson's *Hennes ord: Värk I–III* (2019; Her Words: Ache I–III).[2] The novels are selected to give diverse perspectives on involuntary childlessness; they represent different genres (autofiction and popular fiction), and the protagonists have different life situations: one lives in a heterosexual relationship (Glaser), one is single, at least in the beginning of the novel (Haag), and one is in a lesbian relationship (Folkesson).

Pernilla Glaser's novel depicts Emma, who is in her late thirties and tries to become pregnant with her male partner Jimpa. They have struggled to have children for four years and gone through two fertility treatments. They both work as architects, but while Jimpa has thrown himself into a promising career, Emma's career has stalled. The novel depicts Emma's life crisis, which plays out in relation to different gendered and heterosexual norms.

Martina Haag's novel centers on forty-four-year-old Nadja, who is on the waitlist to adopt as a single woman. Nadja receives news from the adoption agency about new regulations that will prioritize married couples, which eliminates her chances to adopt. She makes a deal with her sister, Lotta, who will find a man Nadja can marry if Nadja takes care of Lotta's father-in-law, Sigvard, while Lotta and her husband go on a trip to Paris to save their marriage. Through a misunderstanding Nadja is put in contact with the wrong man, Jocke, but against all odds Nadja and Jocke fall in love. They decide to get married, but when Jocke finds out about Nadja's need to marry someone in order to adopt, he feels betrayed and leaves Nadja at the altar. After some time apart the couple reunite at the end of the novel and get married.

Tove Folkesson's autofictional novel depicts the writer Tove and her partner Hanna, who struggle to become parents through donor insemination while building a life on the countryside near Tove's maternal grandmother and uncle's farm, which has been in the family for generations. During the course of the novel, Tove and Hanna go through two inseminations; the first is initially successful, as Tove gets pregnant, but it ends in miscarriage, and the second fails.

---

[2] These novels have not been translated into English, so all translations are my own in collaboration with line editor Rebecca Ahlfeldt.

## "But I Just Wanted to Be Normal": Normative Femininity and the Swedish Gender Equality Ideal

Motherhood is constructed as the core of femininity, and women who have chosen not to become mothers are often viewed as unfeminine (see, for instance, Cummins et al. 2021; Peterson and Fjell 2010, 124–25). The novels discussed in this chapter do not depict women who are voluntarily childless but women who struggle to become mothers. However, the novels still highlight how the protagonists in various ways negotiate normative femininity. To some extent, their status as childless women seems to be a threat to their femininity, but the link between femininity and motherhood is also criticized and undermined in the novels. In this section I will discuss how the three novels' representations of femininity play out against the backdrop of the Swedish gender equality ideal and Swedish pronatalism.

The three novels are published in a Swedish context, where gender equality is conceptualized as a national characteristic (see, for instance, Martinsson et al. 2016). Gender equality has been a core value of the Swedish welfare state, and it is linked to the possibility of combining professional and family life. With the expansion of the public sector after the Second World War, many Swedish women entered the labor market, which in turn led to demands for political measures that would make it possible for women to be working mothers. During the 1970s the social-democratic government launched an ambitious political program aiming at gender equality, with state-subsidized affordable childcare and generous paid parental leave for both mothers and fathers. The Swedish gender equality ideal requires both parents to contribute to the labor market and also to care for their children, thus promoting a dual-earner/dual-carer ideal (see, for instance, Björk 2017; Gottzén and Jonsson 2012; Klinth 2002; Klinth and Johansson 2010; Martinsson et al. 2016). In Swedish politics and public debate, gender equality is usually viewed as an unquestioned goal, and analyzing and critiquing gendered norms and structures are steps in the process of achieving this goal (see, for instance, Dahl 2005).

Swedish gender equality politics is interlinked with progressive family politics as many of the reforms initiated from the 1970s and onward facilitate the combination of career and family life. Through various political measures, the Swedish welfare state has encouraged its citizens to reproduce, at least since the 1930s when birth rates in Sweden fell to a record low. Initially these measures were explicitly pronatalist, as they aimed to increase birth rates. Today Sweden's progressive family politics does not explicitly aim at increasing birth rates, but as I have argued elsewhere, it still has pronatalist dimensions and contributes to pronatalist pressure (Björklund 2021, 191–93, 236–37). Compared to other European countries, Sweden also has high birth rates.

Glaser's novel ties into a Swedish gender equality discourse by highlighting and problematizing how gender roles and gendered structures saturate both professional and personal lives. Emma's and Jimpa's different positions in the job market are a recurring theme. While they were in school together, Emma was the smarter and more hard-working of the two, and everybody had expected her, rather than Jimpa, to get a top job after graduation (Glaser 2010, 129, 220). Emma connects the facts that Jimpa has a better job and a higher salary to gender: "He was a promising young man and she was a diligent girl. There's a difference" (Glaser 2010, 30).[3] Gender roles and gendered structures are also visible in the couple's personal lives, especially in their responses to involuntary childlessness. Jimpa pulls away, invests in work, and does not want to talk about the process. Emma is unhappy, and the struggle to have children rules her life. As with gendered structures in professional life, Emma connects some of the differences to gender. She remembers how, as a little girl, she used to play a game that would tell her how many children she would have as an adult: "Emma had once asked Jimpa if he had played that game as a child. He had snorted and laughed and said that little boys don't think about having children. Emma assumed that both little boys and little girls thought about what their adult life would look like. But in order to visualize an adult woman you apparently had to visualize a parent" (Glaser 2010, 81).[4] Here Emma's awareness of gender serves a didactic purpose, pointing to how femininity is culturally constructed as linked to motherhood, while masculinity is not linked to fatherhood. Similarly, Emma's critique of the view of the female body as either maternal or an object for men's desire is conveyed in an ironic or humorous way, when she imagines what it is like to have a baby: "What a relief. You could wear a milk-stained college sweatshirt all day and everyone would still find you radiantly

---

[3] "Han var en påläggskalv och hon var en duktig flicka. Det var skillnad."
[4] "Emma hade frågat Jimpa en gång om han hade lekt den leken när han var liten. Han hade fnyst och skrattat och sagt att småkillar tänker väl inte att de ska ha barn. Emma antog att både småkillar och småtjejer tänkte på hur det skulle bli när de blev vuxna. Men för att tänka sig en vuxen kvinna behövde man tydligen tänka sig en förälder."

beautiful and fresh-looking since you were a Mother with a sacred task" (Glaser 2010, 31).[5] She makes clear that as motherhood is positioned at the core of femininity, there is less need for a mother to make an effort to look beautiful in order to perform normative femininity.

The examples above can be understood as the novel writing itself into a Swedish gender equality discourse, in which critiques of gendered structures and stereotypes are part of the process to achieve gender equality. Gendered norms and the link between femininity and motherhood are also critiqued in Haag's novel, though in a slightly different way. While Glaser's Emma still adapts to normative femininity by making motherhood the sole purpose of her life, Haag's Nadja is different. She is into heavy metal and confidently maneuvers Jocke's snowmobile; when Jocke asks if she can do it, she responds: "Of course I can. I've had a driver's license for a [motor] bike since I was sixteen. How much harder can it be to drive one of these?" (Haag 2011, 171).[6] Heavy metal, motorcycles, and snowmobiles are conventionally masculine domains, and by embracing them Nadja represents a less conventional femininity. In other ways, Nadja's femininity does not depart too much from the Swedish gender equality ideal. Ulrika Dahl argues that Swedish gender equality politics has aimed at changing the division of labor between women and men—to redefine what both groups can do. But even if men can do household work and women can fix a car, they are not supposed to deviate too much from normative gender roles, as the Swedish gender equality ideal is based on heteronormativity, according to which genders are binary, separate, opposite and supposed to desire each other (Dahl 2005). Similarly, in Haag's novel Nadja can drive a snowmobile, but she still dresses in a conventionally feminine way, with high-heeled boots, thin leather gloves, and a purse.

However, in Haag's novel the link between femininity and motherhood is undermined through humor and performativity. Feminist theory (see, for instance, Butler 1999 [1990]; Lundberg 2008; Österholm 2012) has highlighted how norms of femininity and patriarchal and heteronormative structures can be resisted with the use of humor, failure, and excess. Anna

---

[5] "Vilken befrielse. Man kunde gå runt i en mjölkfläckig collegetröja hela dagen och alla tyckte ändå att man var så strålande vacker och fräsch eftersom man var moooor med ett heligt uppdrag."

[6] "Klart jag kan. Jag har haft bågekort sedan jag var sexton, det kan ju inte vara mycket svårare att köra en sån här."

Lundberg (2008) shows how excess and laughter are often used in feminist and queer comic culture to challenge oppressive power structures and indicate that a different social order is possible. In Haag's novel, Nadja adapts to a more conventional femininity that is compatible with ideal motherhood when registering at the adoption agency. Humor is used to highlight how her adaptations to conventional femininity and motherhood are done in a performative manner, which reveals the instability of these identities as well as the link between them. Before the visit from Social Services, which is part of her approval process as an adoptive parent, Nadja sews curtains to make her apartment look nice. Curtains and sewing are here framed as part of what is expected of her as a mother-to-be, which indicates that it is a kind of performance of normative femininity (Butler 1999). But, as Judith Butler argues, performing femininity will always fail to some extent, as there is no true or core femininity; rather, it is constructed through various iterations. In Nadja's case, femininity fails, as she is not particularly good at traditionally feminine handicrafts such as sewing and knitting but also because of the way she performs these skills. Her sewing and knitting are excessive; she makes loads of dresses of different sizes as well as pants, sweaters, and pillows in the shape of the whole Barbapapa family (Haag 2011, 18–19).[7] The choice of the Barbapapa family further highlights excess; the family is (too) large, and the members threaten normativity as they constantly shift shapes and can morph into something unexpected. Maria Margareta Österholm (2012) argues that excessive femininity can be subversive, as it reveals the performative dimensions of femininity. Similarly, in Haag's novel, the iterations and the excess call attention to the constructed character of femininity but also of motherhood, as these identities are linked in Nadja's preparations for the adoption. Moreover, since femininity and motherhood are both revealed as constructions, the link between them is destabilized.

Still, even if the link between motherhood and femininity is criticized in Glaser's and Haag's novels, motherhood is connected to a normative life course. Glaser's Emma is depicted as someone who is invested in how she appears to others and in upholding a perfect façade, and her strivings to become a mother are sometimes framed as a means to fulfill norms. When she reflects on why she wants a nuclear family so badly, she cannot find an

[7]The Barbapapa family appears in a series of children's picture books from the 1970s, created by the French-American couple Annette Tison and Talus Taylor. The family members are pear-shaped, blob-like characters who can shift shapes at will.

explanation other than that she wants what everybody else has: "She wanted a husband and children and a car and maybe a little dog. Ski vacations to Sälen [a Swedish ski resort] and summer vacations to Greece and a house that she had designed herself. It was security, perhaps, or at least some kind of community" (Glaser 2010, 15).[8] When Emma imagines what everybody else has, it is a normative, middle-class family life, and this life has the potential to create security and community. She also distances herself from other childless women in the online support groups she sometimes attends: "She didn't want to be one in a group of desperate women. She wanted to be successful" (Glaser 2010, 102).[9] Being able to conceive is here linked to being a successful woman, which means performing normative femininity.

Over the course of the novel Emma's depression escalates, but the turning point comes when she realizes that she has to stop prioritizing the appearance of success over her own happiness. Since appearance and success have been linked to the ability to fulfill norms throughout the novel, this turn of events can be seen as a critique of these norms. The critique is also reinforced by the examples, discussed above, of how gendered norms restrict Emma's life. The representation of Emma shows how she is deeply impacted by these norms. Even if she is critical of the gendered structures that position Jimpa as a promising young man with a thriving career and her as a mother-to-be, she does not apply for a new job. Her solution to her career problems is to hope to become pregnant to be able to go on parental leave (Glaser 2010, 129). Despite her critique of the construction of the female body as either maternal or sexual, she adopts this view of herself and takes on the blame for her and Jimpa's failure in both areas. She hates her body after the fertility treatments have failed (Glaser 2010, 219), and she worries that the lack of love and affection between her and Jimpa is due to her not being sexy enough (Glaser 2010, 130).

Even in Haag's novel, which undermines the link between femininity and motherhood in the most forceful way, the impact of this construction is hard to escape for Nadja. Infertility is sometimes represented as incompatible with femininity, such as when Nadja first finds out about her inability to have children: "Sterile. What a freaking word. Childless.

---

[8] "Hon ville ha man och barn och bil och kanske en liten hund. Skidsemestrar till Sälen och solsemestrar till Grekland och ett eget ritat hus. Det var trygghet kanske eller i alla fall någon sorts gemenskap."

[9] "Hon ville inte vara en i en mängd desperata kvinnor. Hon ville vara lyckad."

Malfunctioning woman. Infertile" (Haag 2011, 8).[10] Nadja is also, to some extent, faulted for being childless: her infertility is said to be caused by untreated chlamydia in her unruly teens (Haag 2011, 74), which suggests that she was not responsible enough to care for her future reproductive capacities.

On the one hand, Glaser's and Haag's novels critique gendered norms and structures and undermine the link between femininity and motherhood, but, on the other hand, motherhood is still placed at the center of a normative life course for women, especially in Glaser's novel. I have discussed how the critique of gendered structures can be read in light of the Swedish gender equality ideal, but the normative position of motherhood can also be situated in the Swedish context as part of Swedish pronatalism. The Swedish welfare state has not only facilitated for women the combination of professional and family life; infertile couples also have access to fertility treatments through the tax-funded health care system. This right was extended to lesbian couples in 2005 and to single women in 2016. Rikke Andreassen (2019, 85) has argued that non-normative families do not necessarily undermine traditional family ideals but, rather, extend those ideals to include new types of family members. I would argue that the same could be said of motherhood; as the Swedish state has granted reproductive rights to more groups, the normative position of motherhood is strengthened.

The normative positioning of motherhood is even more pronounced in Folkesson's novel, as motherhood becomes a way for the protagonist Tove to become "normal" and compensate for non-normative sexuality. Folkesson's novel does not challenge the link between femininity and motherhood to the same extent as Glaser's and Haag's, even if it sometimes questions concepts of what is natural. The idea of conception as natural is resisted, sometimes even explicitly, such as when Tove responds to Hanna's fear of people who think conception should happen "naturally" by pointing out that there is nothing natural—"everything has been created by us" (Folkesson 2019, 114).[11] The idea of what is seen as natural is also problematized through the many connections between, on the one hand, Tove and Hanna's relationship and their struggle to become parents and, on the other hand, nature and farming, such as in a passage where it

[10] "Steril. Vilket jävla ord. Barnlös. Icke fungerande kvinna. Ofruktsam."
[11] "Allt har vi skapat."

is stated that "most cows are inseminated" (Folkesson 2019, 132).[12] Nature imagery is also prominent in the depiction of the insemination, as when Tove lets her entire body "become big and wet like a field, and the light inhale, the blue-white drop of life" (Folkesson 2019, 180).[13] Connecting lesbianism to the natural world is a common trope in lesbian literature, and it serves to counter discourses of same-sex love as against nature (Bergdahl 2010; Björklund 2014).

However, while the discourse on lesbianism as against nature is challenged in Folkesson's novel, the idea of "the natural" as acceptable and "normal" is upheld. Several times Tove mentions the shame she feels about not being able to conceive without help (Folkesson 2019, 23, 44, 68), which frames this process as something that should happen within a very narrow definition of "naturally." Similar normalizing strategies appear throughout the novel, such as the many connections to the Bible and Virgin Mary. The chapter when Tove and Hanna receive the letter from the hospital about their first appointment contains several explicit references to the Annunciation, such as Mary, Joseph, and the archangel Gabriel, as well as verbatim quotes from the Bible. The recurring references to Mary highlight how an unconventional pregnancy where no man has been involved can still make the mother the symbol of all mothers and serves to normalize Tove's motherhood.[14]

Motherhood is also represented as a way for Tove to *become* "normal." She thinks about herself as deviant in relation to all the women who have lived on the farm: "But I just wanted to be normal. Give birth, like them. Care. Be a regular mother" (Folkesson 2019, 19).[15] Motherhood even seems to compensate for non-normative sexuality, as Tove hopes that being pregnant will make her more familiar and easier to accept among her countryside neighbors (Folkesson 2019, 219). While motherhood is linked to normality, childlessness is connected to deviance. Tove refers to a story about a childless widow who used to live nearby and is said to haunt the neighborhood. Tove wonders whether the widow was a lunatic who failed to become pregnant and hopes that she herself will not end up like the widow (Folkesson 2019, 217–19). Tove's fear of childlessness is a

---

[12] "De flesta kor insemineras."

[13] "bli stor och blöt som en åker, och den ljusa inandningen, blåvita droppen liv."

[14] It also further strengthens the idea of motherhood as sacred, which is particularly interesting in relation to Sweden's status as one of the world's most secularized countries (Berggren and Trägårdh 2006, 383).

[15] "Men jag ville bara vara normal. Föda, som de. Vårda. Vara en vanlig mor."

recurring theme in the novel, especially after the miscarriage; it is associated with shame (Folkesson 2019, 372), exclusion (Folkesson 2019, 395–96), and fear of not being able to carry on the family line (Folkesson 2019, 371). Parenthood is also connected to success; when comparing being a writer to being a parent, Tove concludes that being a parent is linked to higher status (Folkesson 2019, 357). Tove's struggle to become "normal" through having children firmly positions motherhood at the core of normativity.

The representations of femininity and non-motherhood in Glaser's, Haag's, and Folkesson's novels have to be read in the Swedish context, where family politics is closely tied to the gender equality ideal. While the novels sometimes explicitly critique gendered structures and the link between femininity and motherhood, thus becoming part of a Swedish gender equality discourse, they also, to various extents, reinstate motherhood at the core of femininity, in line with Swedish pronatalism. Moreover, all three novels center on a woman who wants to become a mother and follow her perspective closely. Their partners are represented only from the women's point of view, which gives limited insight into their thoughts and feelings around infertility. The dominant position these novels give to the woman who gives birth further strengthens the link between femininity and motherhood.

## "I Want Children Too, but Together with Him": Nuclear Families and Heteronormative Temporality

The Swedish gender equality ideal, with its links to family politics and the dual-earner/dual-carer model, is intertwined with normative heterosexuality and the nuclear family norm (see, for instance, Björklund 2021; Dahl 2005). These norms are also tied to (hetero)normative temporality. Jack Halberstam (2005) argues that the Western world constructs respectability and normality according to "a middle-class logic of reproductive temporality" (4) based on "those paradigmatic markers of life experience—namely, birth, marriage, reproduction, and death" (2). For Halberstam, reproductive temporality is a heteronormative construction, but it still guides the way we are expected to lead our lives, what counts as a good life and the order the markers of life experiences should follow. Glaser's, Haag's, and Folkesson's novels depict involuntary childlessness, and as such, they represent a kind of stalled (hetero)normative temporality. The protagonists are stuck in time, waiting to move on with their lives and enter into a new life stage as mothers. The novels also disrupt the nuclear family ideal, since the protagonists are unable to reproduce. However, as I will show, the novels, to some extent, also confirm these ideals. In this section, I will discuss how the three novels relate to the nuclear family norm and the logics of (hetero)normative temporality.

Haag's novel, and to some extent Glaser's, explicitly resists the nuclear family norm. In Haag's novel, this norm is often supported by other characters, such as when a worker at the adoption agency, explaining the decline of Nadja's application, tells her that the adoption agency needs to think about what is best for the children: "now the child will go to a married couple instead, with both a mother and a father" (Haag 2011, 49).[16] The nuclear family norm is also upheld through the recurring representations of childlessness as linked to loneliness and emptiness, such as when Nadja first receives the bad news from the adoption agency: "I am 44 years old and childless. I will be alone for the rest of my life. In fifty years, I will be dead. In a hundred years, nobody will know that I have even existed" (Haag 2011, 55; see also 44–46, 71, 144).[17] However, while the nuclear family often is referred to explicitly as the best way to lead one's life, such as in the example at the adoption agency above, it is represented in a less rosy light. This is sometimes done through comedic contrasts. Nadja's mother constantly nags Nadja because she is single and childless and compares her to her sister Lotta, who got married early and had three children. She tells Nadja how happy Lotta is and how Lotta knows "how to have a REALLY GOOD LIFE!" (Haag 2011, 25).[18] In the chapter that follows, Lotta is introduced for the first time, and it turns out that her life is not as great as their mother portrays it; her marriage is unhappy, and Lotta is in charge of all the unpaid household work: the house, the children, and her father-in-law, who orders her around and complains about everything. Nadja and Lotta's mother is represented as a comical stereotype who literally speaks in capitals when delivering her "truths" about what a good life entails, and the contrast between the flawless façade she tries to uphold and Lotta's unhappy nuclear family life creates a comedic effect and

---

[16] "nu får ju barnet komma till ett gift par istället, med både en mamma och en pappa."
[17] "Jag är 44 år och barnlös. Jag kommer att leva ensam i resten av mitt liv. Om femtio år är jag död. Om hundra år är det ingen som vet att jag ens har levat."
[18] "hur man ska ordna ett RIKTIGT BRA LIV!"

suggests that having husbands and children may not make women happy after all.

The nuclear family norm is also resisted through contrasts between the novel's representations of nuclear families and other relationships. There are very few representations of happy nuclear families in the novel. Lotta and her husband travel to Paris to save their marriage, but start fighting again shortly after their return. Nadja and Lotta have a complicated relationship with their mother, and the novel does not mention their father. Nadja's best friend Katti is divorced and has shared custody of her children. However, other relationships are represented as more resilient. Nadja's relationship with Katti is depicted as closer than any of the more conventional family bonds in the novel. When Katti hears that Nadja will not be able to adopt, she is in a TV studio recording a show, but she fakes food poisoning in order to support her friend. She encourages Nadja to find someone to marry and runs Nadja's sound studio while she is away. Katti appears more reliable than any of Nadja's family members, and the representation of Nadja and Katti's relationship thus counters Nadja's fear of having a lonely childless life. The novel also represents the bond between Lotta's father-in-law Sigvard and Jocke as close and loving, and when Nadja develops a relationship with both of them, the three form a kind of family bond even if neither one of them is (genetically) related.

Nadja's relationship with Katti and her relationship with Jocke and Sigvard come across as happier and more stable than the nuclear families depicted in the novel. Moreover, children are rarely represented, and when they are, they are mostly depicted as annoying. Also, when Nadja falls in love with Jocke, the love for Jocke rather than reproduction becomes her priority. She even turns down two marriage proposals to be with him; she declines Sigvard's offer to marry her when Jocke has left and turns down the man whom Lotta originally set her up with and who appears at the doorstep when Nadja has fallen in love with Jocke but before they decide to get married. In a phone call Katti asks Nadja if she has given up on having a child, and Nadja responds, "No, but what's most important right now is Jocke. I want to be with him. Whether we have children or not, we'll see, but in that case, we will adopt together. I want Jocke. I want children too, but together with him" (Haag 2011, 235).[19] Jocke also

---

[19] "Nej, men det viktigaste av allt just nu är faktiskt Jocke. Jag vill vara med honom. Om det blir barn eller inte får vi se, men i såna fall ska vi adoptera det tillsammans. Jag vill ha Jocke. Barn vill jag också ha, men då tillsammans med honom."

chooses Nadja over reproduction; when she tells him she is infertile before they get married at the end of the novel, he responds that it is okay since they have reindeer.[20] Nadja and Jocke do not have children at the end of the novel, though Nadja receives a letter from the adoption agency on the last page.

The ending of Glaser's novel challenges the nuclear family norm in a similar way. Emma and Jimpa have a conversation where Jimpa admits that he, too, grieves their inability to have children, and at the end of the novel their relationship is better than ever. Even though they acknowledge that they both want to have children, they do not make any concrete plans for new fertility treatments, and the novel ends with the restored intimacy between Emma and Jimpa, which reinforces something Jimpa has said earlier in the novel: "We are already a family. We do not need a child to prove that" (Glaser 2010, 204).[21] Thus, the novel's ending showcases other ways of being a complete family and highlights Emma's happiness with this family constellation.

Similar to Haag's, Folkesson's novel challenges the nuclear family norm by representing other ways of organizing close relationships. Tove resists the idea of the nuclear family as the only way to happiness and community, like when she thinks about her uncle Arne who is not alone even if he had led his adult life without a nuclear family of his own (Folkesson 2019, 41). The novel also sets up an alternative to the nuclear family: Tove, Hanna, the grandmother, and Arne form a kind of family, and they care for each other. When Arne needs to go to the hospital for cancer treatment, Tove takes him, and Tove and Hanna care for grandmother and the farm while he is away. Arne, who is a hunter, makes sure Tove and Hanna have a supply of meat. When they all have tea together in grandmother's kitchen, Tove refers to them as a family: "Grandmother looks so happy because we will stick together when she dies. A strange little family consisting of two + uncle + dog" (Folkesson 2019, 99).[22] Here the dog is also included in the family, and while grandmother is not, since she will soon die, she is part of the community in the present.

At first glance, Folkesson's novel also challenges heteronormativity by representing a lesbian couple. As mentioned above, lesbian couples have

---

[20] Jocke belongs to the indigenous Sámi population and owns reindeer.
[21] "Vi är redan en familj. Det behöver vi väl inte ett barn för att bevisa."
[22] "Mormor ser så glad ut för att vi håller ihop, när hon ska dö. En liten märklig familj om två + morbror + hund."

had access to assisted reproduction in the tax-funded Swedish health care system since 2005, and, similar to gender equality, a progressive attitude about LGBTQI+ issues can be seen as a kind of Swedish-branded value. However, as Ulrika Dahl (2018) argues, only a particular kind of lesbian mother figure is accepted and celebrated in the Swedish context: "Cast in white cis-gendered femininity, this figure is entangled in homonationalist ideas about gender equality and sexual exceptionalism that extend rather than challenge heteronormative white middle-class kinship ideals" (1034). The concept of homonationalism was coined by Jasbir K. Puar (2017), who builds on Lisa Duggan's term homonormativity, which refers to a neoliberal gay politics which rests on domesticity and consumption and does not challenge heteronormativity, but instead maintains and supports it. Puar uses homonationalism to describe how sexual exceptionalism is linked to the nation and regulates who is excluded from the national imaginary: "this brand of homosexuality operates as a regulatory script not only of normative gayness, queerness, or homosexuality, but also of the racial and national norms that reinforce these sexual subjects. There is a commitment to the global dominant ascendancy of whiteness" (2).

Folkesson's novel reproduces homonationalism by depicting how Tove and Hanna, as a white, cis-gendered, middle-class couple, can take advantage of Sweden's lesbian-inclusive reproductive laws and by linking sexual exceptionalism to Swedish whiteness. As discussed above, the novel's use of nature imagery counters the discourse of lesbianism as against nature, but, at the same time, the positioning of Tove and Hanna and their reproductive process in a traditional Swedish farming landscape reinforces homonationalist ideas of Swedishness, visible also in other cultural representations of white Swedish lesbian couples (Dahl 2018). The connection to Swedishness and whiteness is underscored in other passages, such as when Tove thinks about the child she will have as being legitimized by the state (Folkesson 2019, 204) or when it is stated, repeatedly, that the donor will be a nice guy, a Swede with blue eyes (Folkesson 2019, 125, 173–74, 176), and these passages also link sexual exceptionalism to the nation and Swedish pronatalism. Moreover, Tove's struggle to become "normal" through having children, discussed in the previous section, does not really challenge heteronormativity but, rather, supports it. As such, the novel reproduces and extends certain "heteronormative white middle-class kinship ideals" (Dahl 2018, 1034), but it can also be said to reinforce (hetero)normative temporality, as parenthood is represented as key to a normative life course.

Glaser's and Haag's novels, which also depict white, middle-class protagonists, reproduce (hetero)normative temporality in a more forceful
way, as they position reproduction within a heterosexual framework. At
one point in Glaser's novel Jimpa tells Emma that he wants to stop trying
to have children, and she considers leaving him to increase her chances of
becoming a mother (Glaser 2010, 64, 119).[23] But for Emma the heterosexual relationship and children are linked; she wants Jimpa and her to
fight together to have a family (Glaser 2010, 64). Emma learns to be content with her relationship instead of leaving Jimpa to pursue motherhood
on her own, which confirms (hetero)normative temporality, according to
which reproduction should not happen out of coupledom. Similarly,
instead of pursuing motherhood on her own, Haag's Nadja focuses on
getting married and finding a father for her future children. The ending of
Haag's novel can be read in the Scandinavian context where the dual-
earner/dual-carer and involved fatherhood ideals are prevalent and where
research shows how single motherhood by choice is seen as a Plan B when
women have been unable to find a man (Andreassen 2019, 66, 93; Bodin
et al. 2021; Henriksson and Bergnehr 2021). Both Glaser's Emma and
Haag's Nadja choose the prospect of reproduction within a heterosexual
framework over pursuing single motherhood, thus reinforcing Swedish
family norms as well as (hetero)normative temporality.

In many ways Glaser's, Haag's, and Folkesson's novels undermine the
nuclear family ideal; they critique it and represent alternatives. Moreover,
none of the novels ends with children or even a pregnancy, which disrupts
the nuclear family ideal and (hetero)normative temporality. At the same
time, by positioning motherhood as key to a normative life course and
reproduction within a heteronormative framework, they also reproduce
these ideals.

## CONCLUSION: CHALLENGING THE MIRACLE-BABY-IN-THE-END NARRATIVE

Glaser's, Haag's, and Folkesson's novels represent involuntary childlessness from three different perspectives—one protagonist is in a heterosexual relationship, one is single, and one is a lesbian. The books also belong
to different genres; Glaser's and Haag's novels are popular literature,

---

[23] The reader is never informed of the medical reason for the couple's infertility, and Emma
considers leaving Jimpa because he retreats from their struggle to have children.

while Folkesson's is critically acclaimed (auto)fiction. Despite the differences in perspective and genre, these novels represent involuntary childlessness in similar ways. They all focus on white, middle-class protagonists, and they all reinforce and challenge norms around femininity and reproduction, as they are conceptualized in the Swedish context.

On the one hand, these representations of non-motherhood illustrate the centrality of motherhood to normative femininity; infertility makes Glaser's Emma and Haag's Nadja feel like malfunctioning women, and Folkesson's Tove hopes that motherhood will make her "normal" and compensate for her non-normative sexuality. The link between motherhood and femininity is, of course, not a Swedish phenomenon, but it takes particular shape in the Swedish context where pronatalist measures date long back and have facilitated motherhood for women, contributing to a kind of mandatory motherhood (Björklund 2021). The novels also represent motherhood as intertwined with heteronormativity; Emma and Nadja choose heterosexual coupledom over pursuing motherhood on their own, and all three novels reinforce heteronormative temporalities by positioning motherhood within the nuclear family and as key to a normative life course.

On the other hand, the novels also resist norms around femininity and reproduction, at least to some extent. In Glaser's novel Emma is critical of the gender structures that both give Jimpa a more promising career and frame parenthood as key to adult femininity but not to adult masculinity. Haag's novel challenges normative femininity by highlighting its performative character through excess and humor, and it resists the normative position of the nuclear family by portraying it as a failing project. Folkesson's and Haag's novels also provide alternatives to the nuclear family: friendships and cross-species families.

However, the novels' most radical and norm-breaking dimension is the fact that none of them ends with children or even a pregnancy. In Glaser's novel Jimpa tells Emma that they do not need a child to prove that they are a family, and even though they both want children when the novel ends, they are not making any plans for new fertility treatments. In Haag's novel Jocke and Nadja do not have children at the end of the novel, and it is unclear what the future holds for them; the last sentence of the novel describes a letter that arrives from the adoption agency, but the novel ends before it is opened. Jocke's response to Nadja also indicates that he is just as happy with a cross-species family consisting of him, Nadja and reindeer. In Folkesson's novel Tove and Hanna plan to continue the fertility treatments, but Tove is not pregnant at the end of the novel. The process around the fertility treatments, including the miscarriage, is depicted in great detail—from the first blood streaks on the toilet paper to the lumps coming out of Tove's vagina. These details together with the fact that the novel does not end with a baby or a pregnancy suggest that experiences of failed fertility treatments can be represented in their own right and not only as steps toward a happy ending.

The letter from the adoption agency in Haag's novel can, of course, be interpreted as an indication of a child-to-be, and in Folkesson's novel, Tove and Hanna will continue trying for a baby. Folkesson's novel is also the first volume of a trilogy in progress, and the second volume (Folkesson 2021) depicts a successful fertility treatment, pregnancy, and the birth of a child. Still, there are no children or pregnancies at the end of these novels. We do not know what the letter from the adoption agency says, and Tove never gets pregnant in Folkesson's first novel. The representations of infertility in the three novels studied thus provide a different picture than the one Rebecca Feasey (2019) has identified in mainstream media: the miracle-baby-in-the-end narrative. Instead, these novels offer narratives that break with the conventional infertility plot line and frame the struggle to become a mother as a story that can be told in its own right. As such they widen the representational space for infertility and non-motherhood.

**Acknowledgments** I am very grateful to those who have given valuable feedback on earlier versions of this text: Maja Bodin as well as the editors of and contributors to this volume, especially those who served as assigned readers at a workshop, Margaretha Fahlgren and Valerie Heffernan. I am also greatly indebted to my line editor Rebecca Ahlfeldt.

## References

Andreassen, Rikke. 2019. *Mediated Kinship: Gender, Race and Sexuality in Donor Families.* London and New York: Routledge.
Archetti, Cristina. 2019. No Life Without Family: Film Representations of Involuntary Childlessness, Silence and Exclusion. *International Journal of Media & Cultural Politics* 15 (2): 175–196.
Bergdahl, Liv Saga. 2010. *Kärleken utan namn: Identitet och (o)synlighet i svenska lesbiska romaner.* Umeå: Institutionen för kultur- och medievetenskaper, Umeå universitet.

Berggren, Henrik, and Lars Trägårdh. 2006. *Är svensken människa? Gemenskap och oberoende i det moderna Sverige.* Stockholm: Norstedts.

Björk, Sofia. 2017. *Gender and Emotions in Family Care: Understanding Masculinity and Gender Equality in Sweden.* Gothenburg: University of Gothenburg.

Björklund, Jenny. 2014. *Lesbianism in Swedish Literature: An Ambiguous Affair.* New York: Palgrave Macmillan.

———. 2021. *Maternal Abandonment and Queer Resistance in Twenty-First-Century Swedish Literature.* New York: Palgrave Macmillan.

Björnberg, Ulla. 2016. Nordic Family Policies in a European Context. *Sociology and Anthropology* 4 (6): 508–516.

Bodin, Maja, Charlotta Holmström, Lars Plantin, Lone Schmidt, Søren Ziebe, and Eva Elmerstig. 2021. Preconditions to Parenthood: Changes over Time and Generations. *Reproductive BioMedicine and Society Online* 13: 14–23.

Butler, Judith. (1990) 1999 *Gender Trouble: Feminism and the Subversion of Identity.* New York and London: Routledge.

Cummins, Helene, Julie Ann Rodgers, and Judith Dunkelberger Wouk, eds. 2021. *The Truth about (M)otherhood: Choosing to Be Childfree.* Bradford: Demeter Press.

Dahl, Ulrika. 2005. Scener ur ett äktenskap: Jämställdhet och heteronormativitet. In *Queersverige*, ed. Don Kulick, 48–71. Stockholm: Natur & Kultur.

———. 2018. Becoming Fertile in the Land of Organic Milk: Lesbian and Queer Reproductions of Femininity and Motherhood in Sweden. *Sexualities* 21 (7): 1021–1038.

de Boer, Marjolein Lotte, Cristina Archetti, and Kari Nyheim Solbraekke. 2019. In/Fertile Monsters: The Emancipatory Significance of Representations of Women on Infertility Reality TV. *Journal of Medical Humanities.* Published online 6 April 2019.

Esping-Andersen, Gøsta. 2016. *Families in the 21st Century.* Stockholm: SNS Förlag.

Feasey, Rebecca. 2019. *Infertility and Non-Traditional Family Building: From Assisted Reproduction to Adoption in the Media.* Cham: Palgrave Macmillan.

Folkesson, Tove. 2019. *Hennes ord: Värk I–III.* Stockholm: Bonnier.

———. 2021. *Den stora kyrkan.* Stockholm: Bonnier.

Folkhälsomyndigheten. 2019. *Sexuell och reproduktiv hälsa och rättigheter (SRHR) i Sverige 2017.* Resultat från befolkningsundersökningen SRHR2017. Folkhälsomyndigheten.

Glaser, Pernilla. 2010. *40 minus.* Stockholm: Bonnier.

Gottzén, Lucas, and Rickard Jonsson. 2012. Goda män och Andra män. In *Andra män: Maskulinitet, normskapande och jämställdhet*, ed. Lucas Gottzén and Rickard Jonsson, 7–23. Malmö: Gleerups.

Graham, Melissa, and Stephanie Rich. 2014. Representations of Childless Women in the Australian Print Media. *Feminist Media Studies* 14 (3): 500–518.

Haag, Martina. 2011. *Glada hälsningar från Missångerträsk: En vintersaga.* Stockholm: Piratförlaget.

Halberstam, Judith Jack. 2005. *In a Queer Time and Place: Transgender Bodies, Subcultural Lives.* New York and London: New York University Press.

Henriksson, Helena Wahlström, and Disa Bergnehr. 2021. Reluctantly Solo? Representations of Single Mothers via Donor Procedure, Insemination and IVF in Swedish Newspapers. In *Single Parents: Representations and Resistance in an International Context*, ed. Berit Åström and Disa Bergnehr, 215–234. Singapore: Springer Nature Singapore.

Klinth, Roger. 2002. *Göra pappa med barn: Den svenska pappapolitiken 1960–95.* Umeå: Boréa.

Klinth, Roger, and Thomas Johansson. 2010. *Nya svenska fäder.* Umeå: Boréa.

Lundberg, Anna. 2008. *Allt annat än allvar: Den komiska kvinnliga grotesken i svensk samtida skrattkultur.* Göteborg and Stockholm: Makadam.

Martinsson, Lena, Gabriele Griffin, and Katarina Giritli Nygren. 2016. Introduction: Challenging the Myth of Gender Equality in Sweden. In *Challenging the Myth of Gender Equality in Sweden*, ed. Lena Martinsson, Gabriele Griffin, and Katarina Giritli Nygren, 1–22. Bristol: Policy Press.

Österholm, Maria Margareta. 2012. *Ett flicklaboratorium i valda bitar: Skeva flickor i svenskspråkig prosa från 1980 till 2005.* Stockholm: Rosenlarv.

Peterson, Helen, and Tove Ingebjørg Fjell. 2010. Bilden av frivillig barnlöshet i media. In *Frivillig barnlöshet: Barnfrihet i en nordisk kontext*, ed. Kristina Engwall and Helen Peterson, 105–161. Stockholm: Dialogos and Institutet för Framtidsstudier.

Puar, Jasbir K. 2017. *Terrorist Assemblages: Homonationalism in Queer Times.* Tenth Anniversary Expanded Edition. Durham: Duke University Press.

Statistics Sweden. 2020. *Utan barn: Skillnader i barnlöshet mellan kvinnor och män i olika grupper.* Demografiska rapporter 2020:1. Stockholm: Statistics Sweden.

CHAPTER 5

# Orality/Aurality and Voice of the Voiceless Mother in Abla Farhoud's *Happiness Has a Slippery Tail*

## Eglė Kačkutė

First-person narratives of mothering written from the perspective of monolingual migrant mothers who almost exclusively speak their own native language to their children are exceptionally few.[1] The novel

This publication has received funding from the European Union's Horizon 2020 research and innovation programme under grant agreement No 952366, and from the Centre for Gender Research and the Department of Literature at Uppsala University.

[1] I refer here to Gill Rye's definition of narratives of mothering: "Literary texts where the mother is herself either the first-person narrative subject or, in the first-person narratives, the figure whose point of view is paramount" (2009, 17).

E. Kačkutė (✉)
Department of French Philology, Vilnius University, Vilnius, Lithuania
e-mail: egle.kackute-hagan@flf.vu.lt

© The Author(s) 2023                                                                  77
H. Wahlström Henriksson et al. (eds.), *Narratives of Motherhood and Mothering in Fiction and Life Writing*, Palgrave Macmillan Studies in Family and Intimate Life,
https://doi.org/10.1007/978-3-031-17211-3_5

*Happiness Has a Slippery Tail* (1998) (*Le bonheur a la queue glissante*)[2] by the Canadian Quebecois author of Lebanese origin, Abla Farhoud, is a remarkable and rare example. The novel is an important part of the Quebecois literature and one of the key texts of migrant writing in Quebec. As such, it has been widely researched and interpreted through the lens of *écriture migrante*,[3] as a rich and valuable reflection on the issues of immigrant identity, belonging, transculturality, and mobility especially from the feminist point of view. This chapter reads the novel in light of critical motherhood studies and feminist philosophy as an exploration of what it means to mother in a language that is perceived as foreign by one's children and the community one lives in; what it means to mother in a country the language of which one does not speak and whose social and cultural norms one does not fully understand. One of the most important objectives of this chapter is to theorise the formal literary narrative representation of the voice of a seemingly voiceless migrant mother who is silent in the language of the host country.

To do this, I will use Marianne Hirsch's classic notion of the mother/daughter plot (1989) together with Adriana Cavarero's concept of the double voice that stems from her feminist rereading of the history of philosophy. Cavarero maintains that metaphysics "insists on *what* is Said and never asks after *who* is Saying" (2005, 29), thus privileging mind over body, *semantike* (meaning) over *phone* (voice or sound), and devocalising the *Logos* (word, thought, or speech). As a critique of metaphysics, she uncovers an alternative philosophical and cultural history that focusses on the embodied oral aspects of the saying, on the musicality and the pleasure of speaking, the specificity of each individual voice, and the relationality of the speaker and the listener. Speaking, Cavarero claims, is a fundamentally relational act. Speech fails if there is no one to listen and to respond: "It takes at least a duet, a calling and a responding—or, better, a reciprocal intention to listen, one that is already active in the vocal emission, and that reveals and communicates everyone to the other" (5). Finally, Cavarero

---

[2] Having won a very important France-Québec-Philippe Rossillon literary prize at its publication in 1998 and the France-Quebec Literary Prize in 1999, it went on to become an international best seller and enjoys a positive academic reception. Unless indicated otherwise, translations of quotations are mine.

[3] *Écriture migrante* is a literary phenomenon that emerged in Quebec in the 1980s. It is fiction written by authors born abroad that "is defined by themes related to displacement and hybridity as well as to forms, often tinged with autobiography" ("qui se définit par des thèmes liés au déplacement et à l'hybridité et par des formes particulières, souvent teintées d'autobiographie." Chartier 2002, 305).

locates the uniqueness of every human being in their embodied voice and posits the supremacy of *phone* over *semantike* or the vocality of discourse over its content. She traces that tradition back to Homer, the blind poet, who relies on the muses as a source to his poetry and to the entire oral culture of *epos*. I will apply this theory to read a novel written in French by an author whose first language is Arabic and in which the oral aspect of language, the voice of the mother, is important both structurally and symbolically.

## DOUNIA'S STORY

The novel *Happiness Has a Slippery Tail* tells the story of an illiterate Lebanese migrant woman, Dounia, who is seventy-five years old at the time of the narrative and mother to six children, five of whom are born in Lebanon and one in Montréal. Dounia is born and grows up in Lebanon, in the village Chaghour. She loses her mother as a young child and as a teenager marries her now husband, Salim, whom she found lovable at the time and who, she believes, must have loved her (Farhoud 1998, 43). Leaving Chaghour at the age of seventeen to get married in another village several kilometres away feels like emigration to her (43), and she spends the twelve years in her new home "perceived and feeling as 'a stranger'" (Dahab, 110). It is in that village that she first suffers domestic violence at the hands of her husband Salim. Summoned by her husband, who had emigrated two years previously, Dounia first relocates to Montreal as a young wife and mother of five: Abdallah aged twelve; Samira, Farid, Samir, and Myriam aged four. She is reluctant to go as she rather enjoys life in Lebanon, looking after her children and sustaining the family with the money Salim sends her from Montreal. Salim runs a corner shop in Montreal while living with his estranged mother. After a ten-year stint in Montreal during which Dounia survives a post-partum depression and sees most of her children become adults, she follows her husband to Lebanon for a few years, where she suffers from a reverse culture shock before being forced back to Canada by the civil war. Illiterate and subject to the patriarchal family law that makes social interactions difficult, Dounia never learns French or English. Apart from a few words and broken phrases in French she uses to communicate with her grandchildren, she spends her life in social isolation, cooking and looking after her family. "I don't know how to speak," says Dounia at the beginning of the novel. "I leave it to

Salim. I know how to feed people" (Dahab 2003, 50).[4] With these words the narrator establishes the premises of Dounia's subjectivity—the subjectivity of someone who lives her entire life through others, in utter lack of social agency. Lacking the linguistic means herself, Dounia entrusts her life story to her daughter, Myriam, who writes it in the first person but through Dounia's point of view.

It is perhaps unsurprising that the novel has been read along two conflicting interpretive lines: first, as a story of non-belonging, marginalisation, isolation, lack of subjectivity, and lack of voice (Miraglia 2005; Montandon 2006; Dahab 2009; Maddox 2010; Pruteanu 2012, 2016); second, as a story of subject development and finding or being given a voice. The first interpretive trend is much louder and more pronounced. For example, for Pruteanu, Dounia's (2016) "principal traits of character are her profound silence and resignation" (3) and the only power Dounia maintains is the power she exerts in the kitchen. Elizabeth F. Dahab (2009) frames the narrative as the tale of the mother's solitude and abandonment as well as the story of her loss of voice. The second interpretive trend focusses on ways in which the novel resists Dounia's subjection to silence and social insignificance. Anne Marie Miraglia, for example, claims that although the novel highlights the difficulties of social, cultural, and linguistic integration of migrants in Canada, it also demonstrates that while socially marginalised, Dounia is actually well integrated in the affective family structure. Kate Averis (2017) reads the novel as a story of ongoing self-development, mobility, and transmission. She argues that the home that Dounia reconstructs for herself in Quebec around her children becomes a site of subjective growth for her and her children. Finally, Allison Connolly posits that "[w]hile Dounia was not able to overcome the barriers to integration, her children were" (2017, 41) suggesting that Dounia's children's social success is largely, if not exclusively, due to her mothering.

The one thing all scholars agree about is that the mother-daughter relationship in the novel and the problem of the mother's voice are its central concerns. The dominating view in Farhoud scholarship seems to be that "Myriam desires to give her mother a voice by telling the story of her life" (Connolly 2017, 59). Thus, by the end of the novel Dounia emerges as a "speaking subject" (Pruteanu 2016, 4) whose voice has finally been heard, thanks to her daughter's writing talent. In short, the consensus seems to be that it is the daughter, Myriam, who gives Dounia a voice, thus endowing her with subjectivity.

[4] Translated from French by Jill McDougall.

In this chapter I take issue with this view, arguing that Dounia's story is written in more than one voice, to use Cavarero's expression. I will pick up the interpretive thread laid out by Pruteanu (2012) and Connolly (2017) who both briefly suggest that the novel is at least to some capacity written in Dounia's own voice.

## The Mother's Book

*Happiness Has a Slippery Tail* has an important autobiographical dimension. Farhoud has gone on record saying that the initial chosen title of the novel was going to be *My Mother's Book* further elaborating that the reason why she took up the pen at all was that her mother couldn't (Farhoud quoted by Dahab 2003, 108). Before delving into the textual analysis of the novel, it is important to sketch the story of Farhoud's life that will establish the background of the mother-daughter relationships the novel explores.

Abla Farhoud was born in Lebanon in 1945. She moved to Quebec with her family when she was six in 1951 and attended school in the outskirts of Montreal where her father kept a family store. She was forced to withdraw from high school to help with the store (without pay) so that the family could save enough money to go back to Lebanon, which Farhoud experienced as a deeply gendered injustice (Wimbush 2021). Nevertheless, alongside the heavy duty to her family, she took courses in dramatic art and worked as an actor and speaker for Radio Québec. In 1965, the Farhoud family returned to live in Beirut where Abla worked as a researcher and actor for Radio Lebanon. Talking of her experience of return migration, she remembered feeling appalled by gender inequality in Lebanon where according to her the relationship between the sexes consisted of a battle in which women were always the losers (Delisle and Tézine 2018). In 1969, at the age of twenty, Farhoud left Lebanon for good, this time for Paris where she studied theatre at the Sorbonne. She met her husband, the Quebecois musician, Vincent Dionne, in Paris and returned to Montreal in 1973. Ten years later, while completing an MA in Theatre Arts, Farhoud began to write plays, a shift that she described as a "need to be heard rather than seen" (MacDougall 1999). Listening and speaking as opposed to looking and/or being looked at thus emerge as important concerns for Farhoud as a person and a writer. Since 1973 Farhoud lived and worked in Montreal where she died in 2021.

Arabic is Farhoud's mother tongue in which she was fluent but not fully literate and she called French, the language of writing, her "langue maî-tresse" (Delisle and Tézine 2018), her lover language that she had chosen out of love and in an act of cultural transgression. However, Arabic was the language in which her lifelong relationship with her parents and with her mother in particular happened. It is also the language that nurtured her literary ear. Furthermore, Arab culture is "a culture of orality that has shaped Dounia's world, that oral Arabic wisdom that is a world of strong images, poetry, full of swift ellipses and which is set against the modernity of contemporary America" (Montandon 84).[5] The Arabic oral culture that shaped Dounia's world at least partly shaped Farhoud's literary imaginary and her linguistic sensibilities too. She would have heard her mother use Lebanese expressions and proverbs—traditional ones that are part of the collective culture and probably some that are attributable to her only. Therefore, setting out to write her mother's story, Farhoud likely thought back to and heard her mother's voice in Arabic in her head which she then undertook to translate into literary French or rather Quebecois.

Moreover, the novel *Happiness Has a Slippery Tail* was inspired by Farhoud's childhood memory of watching her mother cry while washing dishes in a Montreal kitchen soon after their arrival to Canada (Delisle and Tézine 2018).[6] As Dahab rightly observes, however, the novel "belongs to the realm of fiction despite the transposition of some of the mother's account [...] mirrored in the *mise en abyme* framework of the novel itself" (108). The autobiographical element of *Happiness Has a Slippery Tail* featuring Farhoud's mother and the fictional character of the work that gives the mother's narrative the first-person perspective makes this text an interesting iteration of the mother/daughter plot as theorized by Marianne Hirsch (1989).

---

[5] "Une culture de l'oralité qui a façonné avec toute sa poésie et sa force le monde de Dounia, cette sagesse arabe orale qui est un monde fortement imagé, poétique, plein de rac-courcis fulgurants et qui s'oppose [...] à la modernité de l'Amérique contemporaine."

[6] There is a fictionalised account of that episode in the novel told from the mother's point of view.

## THE MOTHER/DAUGHTER PLOT AND MIGRANT WOMEN'S WRITING

In her ground-breaking study *The Mother/Daughter Plot* Hirsch posits that the maternal voice in Western culture has been silenced by both patriarchal and some feminist discourses. Hirsch defines the said plot as a story of the subject development and pays especially close attention to the mothers' roles in the stories of daughters' development and to the roles of daughters in stories of mothers' themselves. According to Hirsch, neither mothers nor daughters can do justice to each other's perspectives. When mothers' stories are told by daughters, the mothers are partially silenced and marginalised because what is voiced, is only the mothers' discourse, her story, rather than her full-blown subjectivity and uniqueness. When mothers speak for both themselves and their daughters, they remain objects in their daughters' process of subject-formation. (12) What Hirsch would ideally like to witness in a mother/daughter plot is "mothers and daughters speaking to each other" (8) as two separate, yet deeply connected subjects.

She identifies the black feminist romance as the literary tradition that comes close to achieving this because it is a tradition in which mothers and daughters speak to each other on the grounds of the "racist and sexist oppression which they share" (178). I suggest that in the context of migrant women's writing, mothers and daughters share similar concerns. Oftentimes, mothers and daughters represented in fictions of migration both suffer marginalisation due to their race, ethnicity, and immigrant status. Similarly, they are often both victims of oppressive patriarchal familial structures (albeit to different degrees). In Farhoud's case, for example, she has expressed dismay at being classed as an immigrant author in Quebec despite only ever writing in French and publishing exclusively in Quebec (Zesseu 2015, 17). As previously mentioned, both her mother and she suffered from sexist oppression from Farhoud's father and the Lebanese gender culture more broadly. Farhoud's novel thus shares many traits with the black feminist romance as defined by Hirsch. Using *Happiness Has a Slippery Tail* as a prime example, I suggest that migrant women's writing relies on the "maternal oral tradition of the past" (197), mothers' and daughters' lives are represented as "intertwined with each other" (178), the mothers and daughters do speak to each other, their conversation is anchored in their shared experience of systematic injustice and marginalisation, and mothers speak in two voices, as individual subjects and as mothers (181). In what follows I will demonstrate that in terms of literary representation of the mother's voice, the orality of the mother's voice shines through in the daughter's narrative, the first-person narrative gives Dounia a strong voice, an independent subjectivity, and makes it possible to articulate her mothering experience, especially mothering across the language barrier.

In *Happiness Has a Slippery Tail* Dounia addresses the reader in the first-person singular and "narrates her life to her daughter, Myriam, a prolific writer who realizes that though she has written fifteen books so far, not a single one features her mother. Myriam proceeds to fill this gap in what becomes a project of self-revelation" (Dahab, 108).[7] Thus, the novel stages the subject-formation of the mother. However, the daughter, whom we know to be a fictionalised version of Farhoud, features not only as the enabler in the storytelling but also as a product of Dounia's monolingual mothering. In that sense, the novel stages the mother/daughter plot featuring an imagined conversation between a mother and a daughter who are both fully subjects. The narrative voice in the novel is always that of the mother. However, the narrative perspective is that of the daughter (Farhoud herself) and it is precisely this double dimension that makes the maternal perspective legible to contemporary Western readers. However, Dounia's children, including Myriam, are only represented through Dounia's eyes and with her words putting the mother, the maternal experience, and the voice of the mother centre stage. In this respect, in contrast to Hirsch's suggestion, the daughter functions as an object in the mother's story and maternal subject formation. This narrative device puts the novel *Happiness Has a Slippery Tail* into the category of *matrifocal narratives of migrant mothering*, the genre that tells us most intimately about migrant "mothers' own desires, fears and anxieties, fantasies and imaginative concepts of mothering" (Rye 2009, 3).[8]

Structurally and in terms of the plot, the production of the novel—the oral nature of Dounia's storytelling in Arabic and her daughter's writing it in French—constitutes the essence of the novel. Dounia's and Myriam's lives are represented as intertwined and interdependent. Dounia is loved

---

[7] There is one brief exception to this when at the end of the novel the narrator Dounia refers to herself in the third person in an attempt to represent the complicated self-relations of a person affected by old age-related memory loss.

[8] I coin the term matrifocal narratives of migrant mothering based on Rye's concept of "narratives of mothering" (2009, 17) and Podnieks' and O'Reilly's notion of "matrifocal narratives" (Podnieks and O'Reilly 2010: 3).

and valued in Myriam's house. Myriam's children call her *sitto*, which is an affectionate term for grandmother in Arabic and make her feel like the queen mother. Dounia has exclusive rights at Myriam's house—nobody else is allowed to enter Myriam's study while she writes. Dounia, on the other hand, knows to not overstep the boundaries, she observes her daughter in silence, occasionally serving her coffee, tidying the house, mending children's clothes—in short—creating a favourable environment for her to work in and facilitating her creative work. There are further parallels between their lives. Neither of their marriages has been success-ful—Myriam is recently divorced, while Dounia has been a victim of domestic abuse all her life. Besides, both women are taciturn, pensive, and observant.

Through the intertwining of the mother and daughter characters, "the fusion or confusion" (Hirsch, 1989, 185) of generations occurs. When Dounia watches her daughter work, she sometimes observes Myriam cry and thinks back to herself crying while washing dishes all those years ago, while observed by young Myriam. This in turn makes her think of her own mother who, like Dounia, could not read or write. Having established the transgenerational gendered connection, the novel is quick to introduce the separation between them as a mark of their respective subjectivity. The most pronounced difference being that Myriam, of course, is empowered by her ability to read and write. This is the underlying reason behind Dounia's and Myriam's different behaviour in the face of their broken marriages: Dounia endures and suffers in silence, while Myriam ends the marriage and carries on with her life.

## A MIGRANT MOTHER'S STORY IN MORE THAN ONE VOICE

The most important connection and separation of the two women in the novel lies in their linguistic relationship to one another and to language more broadly. They share their mother tongue, Arabic, which is an oral language for them both: in Dounia's case because she is illiterate, and in Myriam's because she emigrated from Lebanon at the age of four and was schooled in French. Dounia reflects on her linguistic relationship with her daughter: "We both have the same mother tongue, but what with the years she spent learning another language. Myriam lived most of her life here" (24).[9] She recognises that her daughter's linguistic identity is different to hers in two ways. Dounia can only really speak Arabic, whereas Myriam is fluent in French as well as Arabic, and she has also mastered another aspect of language altogether, the written as well as well-spoken French. Cavarero explains that the oral and the written language abide by different organising principles, that speech belongs to the sphere of the ear, whereas writing to the sphere of the eye. The sphere of the ear also comprises the vocal aspect of language, which is sonorous, musical, dynamic, and physical. In contrast, the written language, according to Cavarero, "translates sound and eliminates it" (82). Based on this reasoning, Dounia's linguistic life is that of the ear, whereas Myriam's linguistic self relies more on the sphere of the eye. Her practice as a writer consists of transcribing Dounia's voice into a written system of signification. Nevertheless, Myriam has been initiated into and has some access to her mother's vocal linguistic sensibility.

When Myriam announces to Dounia that she wishes to write a book about her, Dounia accepts the invitation to tell her daughter her story, makes herself comfortable in a rocking chair in Myriam's office, and the difficult process of telling and listening gets underway. The link between Dounia's telling of the story and remembering the details of her past is in line with her belonging to the oral tradition in which the physical production of speech participates in the production of meaning. This is how Dounia experiences her talking sessions with Myriam:

> Every word seems to be important. I can speak as much as I like, without being afraid to make a mistake. With her, my tongue seems to untie itself, my chest breathes better. With others, I can't wait to get to the end of what I am saying, and they can't either. They are right, I am not good with words. With Myriam, I seem to be a different person. (24)[10]

Myriam opens up the space for Dounia where she can engage in the physical act of speaking, in the way of using the organs of speech not only to emit sounds but also to think, to make sense of the story of her life that

---

[9] Nous avons toutes les deux la même langue maternelle, mais que d'années passées à étudier une autre langue. Myriam a vécu presque toute sa vie ici.

[10] Chaque mot a l'air important. Je peux parler autant que je veux, sans peur de me tromper. Avec elle, on dirait que ma langue se délie, que ma poitrine respire mieux. Avec les autres, j'ai toujours hâte d'arriver à la fin et eux aussi. Ils ont raison, je ne sais pas bien parler. Avec Myriam, on dirait que je suis une autre personne.

she is telling. According to Cavarero, "before the advent of metaphysics, it was more natural to believe that thought was a product of the lungs" (62). Similarly, Dounia seems to be using her breathing to comprehend her experience. By engaging in the physicality of her voice, supported with the rhythm and the physicality of a rocking chair, the content of her existence unravels itself. This is also because, rather than listening to the bare linguistic meaning of what she is saying like the others, Myriam listens to Dounia's voice, to the locus of her uniqueness letting Dounia communicate herself to Myriam. As a result, Dounia becomes a different person, from a one-dimensional, ignorant, submissive, and abused woman, she emerges as a fully rounded, complex individual who went through existence making decisions, processing disappointments, considering options, choosing some things over others, and taking responsibility for who she has become.

Since the Homeric epic tradition explored by Cavarero uses sound and rhythms to remember the stories that are being told, it is only natural that Dounia's narrative should culminate in the resurfacing of her traumatic memory from Lebanon. When heavily pregnant Dounia asks Salim to not go away on a business trip as planned but to stay with her for the birth. In response, Salim, already on horseback, kicks her in her face in the presence of her father and children. Furthermore, rather than defending her, Dounia's father takes Salim's side and looks away in silence. The episode is narratively framed as Dounia's internal narrative, prefaced by the elocution: "There are some things you can't say, that should never be spoken to yourself, that should be banished from your thoughts" (Dahab 2003, 61–62). Dounia confesses that her first impulse is to leave Salim, but she then lays out two reasons—one emotional, one practical—as to why she did not. First, leaving Salim would have involved condemning her father to public humiliation due to her violating the patriarchal social order in which they were both steeped. Second, she has nowhere to go, has caring responsibilities, and, considering she is about to give birth, is highly vulnerable. The narrative continues with Dounia expressing painful remorse over not taking action then or later and thus exposing not only herself but her children to continuous domestic violence that has resulted in her eldest son's, Abdallah's, mental illness and her other two sons' delinquency.[11]

---

[11] The scope of this chapter does not allow me to interpret this episode in the light of feminist thinking related to gender-based violence.

Feminist criticism to date tends to read this episode as a sign of Dounia's submissiveness and failure as a woman and a mother. Such readings are predicated on the failure of the maternal narrative voice to discursively transgress the patriarchal law by denouncing it (Miraglia 2005; Dahab 2009). However, the perspective of motherhood studies puts a different spin on this. A careful reading of the novel reveals that the remorse and maternal guilt have been brought about by Myriam's response to Dounia's experience, as illustrated by the following quotation in which Dounia says: "When she picks up on what I've just said with: 'yes, but … you could have … if you wanted to', I see that she cannot put herself in my shoes" (126).[12] It thus becomes clear that Dounia only starts blaming herself because of her interaction with Myriam who, steeped in Western feminism, brought up in a society in which services for gender violence victims exist, but who is also a victim of her mother's failure to stand up to gender-based violence, finds it hard to justify Dounia's behaviour. Maternal guilt and shame are represented through the narrative technique of rhetorical questions the readers guess the answers to (Montandon 2006, 85): "Where could I run? Where could I escape? Where could I go? If my father scorned me and looked the other way, where could I go? [...] Even today, fifty years later, I ask myself why did I not flee, why did I do nothing?" (Dahab 2003, 63). The reader is thus made to realise the impossibility of the task of leaving Salim. Furthermore, the reader is also aware that the novel in which Dounia has the power of the first-person narrative voice is written by Myriam whose emancipated point of view the Western reader identifies with. Contemporary motherhood theory tells us that the culture of blaming mothers for the shortcomings of their mothering, thus making mothers blame themselves, is itself part of the patriarchal ideology (Rose 2018; Phoenix 2011). This novel breaks away from the dominant paradigm of mother blaming in migrant women's writing of the 1970s and 1980s in which migrant mothers' stories were usually told by their writer daughters and through the daughters' narrative voices (Ho 1999). By framing maternal guilt as a cultural and generational difference between the mother and the daughter from the mother's point of view, the novel achieves a more authentic representation of the silent migrant mother's subjectivity. Therefore, as a narrative, the novel takes a sympathetic view towards the mother.

---

[12] "Quand elle reprend ce que je viens de dire en y ajoutant: 'Oui, mais … tu aurais pu … si tu avais voulu', je vois bien qu'elle ne peut pas se mettre à ma place."

## THE POWER OF THE MUSE

The creative collaboration between Dounia and Myriam can be likened to that of a writer and her Muse. In her analysis of Homer's relationship to the Muse, Cavarero explains that Homer functions as a filter between the goddess and the listeners and attributes Homer's power to enchant the audience with his narrative poetry to the workings of the Muse. She claims that Homer "is the only one who can translate the vocality and the omniscience of the Muse into a narrating song" (114). Similarly, Myriam delves into Dounia's orally transmitted story in Arabic and translates it not only into writing but also into literary, poetic, and enchanting French. Myriam is the only one with a privileged access not only to Dounia's story but also to the complexity of her character contained in her speaking voice. Myriam thus enables the telling of Dounia's story, but Dounia gives Myriam the voice, the style, the sound, and the stylistic literary shape to write it with. The structure of the narrative of *Happiness Has a Slippery Tail* is elliptical, non-linear, marked by a particular musicality that is not innately French.

One of the most remarkable features of the novel is the fact that it is sprinkled with Arabic proverbs that appear in the text in French, but that are carefully documented at the end of the novel in both Arabic and French. Dounia often expresses herself with Lebanese proverbs and at more than one point in the narrative, she clarifies that it is easier for her to throw a ready-made phrase in answer to Myriam's difficult questions than trying to formulate a possibly uncomfortable truth about her own life (Farhoud 125). Feminist criticism univocally interprets this as a gendered passivity Dounia has been socialised into. However, Pruteanu accurately remarks that "this linguistic code is only the surface of another language that is the mother's inner language" (2012, 94).[13] The theoretical framework used in this chapter suggests that the proverbs point to the oral tradition Dounia as a storyteller belongs to. Homer "often repeats the same formulas, recombining them," (80) the sonorous modulations of which help him remember the text determining "the very syntax of the verse" (80). In the same way, Dounia repeats the proverbs to remind herself of the story of her life. Repeating the formulaic structures of the proverbs helps her put the events into the wider narrative context of how she might have explained those events to herself at the time of their occurrence. In

---

[13] "Ce code langagier n'est que la surface d'un autre langage intérieur de la mère qui n'a jamais su dire sa peine et ses révoltes."

terms of the textual quality of the novel, those proverbs in translation often break up the French syntax and have the effect of what Russian formalists called defamiliarisation. In the novel, Myriam is represented noting a proverb she had not heard Dounia pronounce before and writing it down in French (35). The list of proverbs at the end of the novel points to a potential real list that Farhoud herself might have kept. It has been argued that through the proverbs Farhoud inscribes her own linguistic and cultural heritage in Quebec's literary landscape (Zesseu 2015; Montandon 2006). However, the list does more than that; it symbolically bridges the gap between the oral and the written cultures which Dounia and Myriam belong to, capturing a fraction of Dounia's and Farhoud's real mother's vibrant sonorous universe and freezing it in writing for posterity.

## Conclusion

In terms of migrant mothering, Dounia claims having not been the same as a mother and as a grandmother. Her mothering is marked by emotional distress, homesickness, and what seems like a clear case of post-partum depression. When her children are young, she longs to speak to their teachers and friends, but is reduced to watching them interact as if separated by an invisible wall eloquently rendered in the novel through multiple scenes in which Dounia watches her children through the window. And yet, her lack of language in French is far from passive or destructive. Rather, it is transformed into a performative act of listening. She creates a space for her children in which they can be themselves and lead lives that they want to lead. Seen from the perspective of Cavarero's concept of the double voice in which speaking is always "a calling and a responding," Myriam's book in French is a response to Dounia's calling in Arabic. Myriam is able to become her unique writer self in French due to Dounia's speaking and listening to her in Arabic. Likewise, Dounia is only able to tell her story and to fully process her life experience due to Myriam's calling.

In short, *Happiness Has a Slippery Tail* is a story in which the mother's and the daughter's voices speak in a duet in which the unique specificity of each voice is communicated and audible. In this way the voice of the silent mother can be heard by the Western readership, and her perspective inscribed in the Western literary tradition. The story is told in two voices: the aural voice of a marginalised mother who is voiceless in French and in writing and that of a French-educated writer daughter who understands the quality of the mother's voice in Arabic. By this narrative token, the voice of the two women becomes political since for the voices of some of the marginalised groups, including illiterate monolingual migrant mothers' voices to be heard, some women must know how to listen and how to translate them in ways that make room for the unique voices of those silent women. Furthermore, the double voice of the daughter-mother duet defies hierarchy. The daughter's perspective that unavoidably mediates the narrative to a degree and that the reader very likely identifies with serves as the sympathetic dimension of the text that withholds judgement and makes for a more nuanced representation of maternal experiences in contemporary fiction.

REFERENCES

Averis, Kate. 2017. Mobility and stasis. Ageing abroad in Abla Farhoud's Le Bonheur a la queue glissante. *Francosphères* 6 (1): 7–20.
Cavarero, Adriana. 2005. *For More Than One Voice. Toward Philosophy of Vocal Expression*. Stanford: Stanford University Press.
Chartier, Daniel. 2002. Les Origines de l'écriture migrante: l'immigration littéraire au Québec au cours des deux derniers siècles. *Voix et Images* 27 (2): 303–316.
Connolly, Allison. 2017. *Spaces of Creation: Transculturality and Feminine Expression in Francophone Literature*. Lexington Books.
Dahab, Elizabeth F. 2003. *Voices in the Desert. An Anthology of Arabic-Canadian Women Writers*. Guernica.
———. 2009. *Voices of Exile in Contemporary Canadian Francophone Literature*. Lexington Books.
Delisle, Monique and Anne-Marie Tézine. 2018. Montreptit entretien avec Abla Farhoud – 26 Septembre, https://www.youtube.com/watch?v=fMnC5_K6_wM (consulted 2021-10-10).
Farhoud, Abla. 1998. *Le bonheur a la queue glissante*. Montréal: L'Hexagone.
Hirsch, Marianne. 1989. *The Mother/Daughter Plot*. Bloomington and Indianapolis: Indiana University Press.
Ho, Wendy. 1999. *In her Mother's House*. Walnut Creek, Oxford: AltaMira.
MacDougall, Jill. 1999. Growing... growing... growing... grown... growing... growing... growing... grown analysis of a work-in-progress. *Women & Performance: a Journal of Feminist Theory* 5 (1): 144–155.
Maddox, Kelly-Anne. 2010. Écrire au centre de soi-même: Le récit identitaire dans l'œuvre romanesque d'Abla Farhoud. *Nouvelles Études Francophones* 25 (2): 128–141.

Miraglia, Anne Marie. 2005. La parole, le silence et l'apprentissage de l'exil dans *Le Bonheur a la queue glissante* d'Abla Farhoud. *Studies in Canadian Literature* 30 (2): 89–95.

Montandon, Alain. 2006. Abla Farhoud: portrait d'une libanaise en exil: à propos du vieillir dans *Le Bonheur à la queue glissante*. *Neohelicon* 33 (1): 81–90.

Phoenix, Ann. 2011. Transforming 'non-normative' motherhood: retrospective accounts of transnational motherhood in serial migration. *Radical Psychology*. 9 (2): 7–17.

Podnieks, Elizabeth, and Andrea O'Reilly, eds. 2010. *Textual mothers/Maternal Texts: Motherhood in Contemporary Women's Literatures*, Waterloo. Ont.: Wilfrid Laurier University Press.

Pruteanu, Simona Emilia. 2012. L'écriture migrante comme pratique signifiante: l'exemple de l'hétérolinguisme et de l'écriture fragmentaire chez Abla Farhoud et Ying Chen. *Nouvelles Études Francophones*. 27 (1): 85–98.

———. 2016. Cooking, Language, and Memory in Farhoud's *Le Bonheur à la queue glissante* and *Thúy's Mãn*. *CLCWeb: Comparative Literature and Culture* 18 (4): 2–6.

Rose, Jacqueline. 2018. *Mothers. An Essay on Love and Cruelty*. London: Faber&Faber.

Rye, Gill. 2009. *Narratives of Mothering: Women's Writing in contemporary France*. Newark: University of Delaware Press.

Wimbush, Antonia. 2021. *Autofiction: A Female Francophone Aesthetic of Exile*. Liverpool University Press.

Zesseu, Claude. 2015. Migration, oralité et altérite dans l'écriture migrante québécoise: le cas d'Abla Farhoud. In *Migrations/Translations*, ed. Ahmed Maroussia, Corinne Alexandre-Garner, Nicholas Serruys, Iulian Toma, and Isabelle Keller-Privat, 241–252. Paris: Presses universitaires de Paris Ouest.

# CHAPTER 6

# From Survivor to Im/migrant Motherhood and Beyond: Margit Silberstein's Postmemorial Autobiography, *Förintelsens Barn*

*Elizabeth Kella*

Those who were in the death camps, the extermination camps, the concentration camps are becoming fewer, but we, their children still exist. I am one of them and I want to tell about my parents, what the Holocaust did to them, what it did to me, we who were not supposed to be. What it means to have taken in our parents' trauma with our mother's milk (190).[1]

This publication has received funding from the European Union's Horizon 2020 research and innovation programme under grant agreement No 952366, and from the Centre for Gender Research and the Department of Literature at Uppsala University.

[1] "De som befann sig i dödslägren, utrotningslägren, koncentrationslägren blir allt färre, men vi, deras barn finns fortfarande kvar. Jag är ett av dem och jag vill berätta om mina föräldrar, vad Förintelsen gjorde med dem, vad den gjort med mig, vi som inte skulle finnas. Vad det innebär att ha fått sina föräldrars trauma med modersmjölken" (190).

E. Kella (✉)
Department of Culture and Education, Södertörn University, Huddinge, Sweden
e-mail: liz.kella@sh.se

© The Author(s) 2023
H. Wahlström Henriksson et al. (Eds.), *Narratives of Motherhood and Mothering in Fiction and Life Writing*, Palgrave Macmillan Studies in Family and Intimate Life,
https://Doi.org/10.1007/978-3-031-17211-3_6

93

In Margit Silberstein's as yet untranslated work of autobiography, *Förintelsens Barn* (Children of the Holocaust) (2021a), the experience of the Holocaust strongly influences the identities and parenting practices of her survivor parents, particularly her mother. Both Ernst Jakob Silberstein and Ili Channe Silberstein (née Grunzweig) were Hungarian-speaking Jews from Transylvania who were alone among their families to survive the Nazi genocide. Ernst survived incarceration in a Soviet labor camp, and Silberstein's mother lived through first Auschwitz, then the death march to the camp in Bergen-Belsen, from which she was liberated in 1945. Ili was transported by the white buses—a rescue attempt organized by the Swedish Red Cross at the end of the war—to Norrköping in Sweden and her fiancé Ernst was reunited with her there in 1948.[2] The two lived and worked in Norrköping most of their lives, where they raised Margit (born 1950) and her younger brother, Willy (born 1954). While Ernst spoke little of his experiences in Siberia, and is represented as a quiet, introverted, and troubled man, Ili told her daughter stories about her pre-war and war experiences and was a central force in the household when Silberstein was growing up. Silberstein's text foregrounds her childhood in this household, and the parental transmission of traumatic Holocaust memory, including the corporeal maternal transmission as suggested in the epigraph by the image of trauma flowing like milk from the mother's breast. The text also represents Silberstein's adult relationship with her mother, and her own maternal relation with her two sons, suggesting that she, too, inadvertently transmits a form of traumatic memory to her offspring, which affects their experience of being Jewish in Sweden.

Silberstein, a prominent journalist who has worked in print, radio, and television, wrote *Förintelsens Barn* after retiring from her work on national public television as a political news commentator and moving on to freelance journalism. The title she selected for her autobiography pays homage to Helen Epstein's groundbreaking work from 1979, *Children of the Holocaust: Conversations with Sons and Daughters of Survivors*, which Silberstein explicitly cites (188). Both title and citation insert Silberstein's text into a tradition inaugurated by Epstein, herself descending from survivors, of children of survivors identifying as members of a distinct

---

[2] For a discussion of the controversy surrounding Sweden's attempt to rescue Scandinavians, cooperating in sending non-Scandinavians to other camps, and widening the rescue attempt to include other imprisoned or interned people only serendipitously, see Kvist Geverts (2020, 2021).

group, frequently referred to as the postmemory generation, with unique experiences of growing up with fathers and mothers profoundly marked by Holocaust trauma.

Silberstein's account, however, also inserts itself into another narrative tradition in which mothers figure strongly: the discourse of im/migration and the emerging discourse of im/migrant or minority literature in Sweden. The term im/migration, incorporating the words "immigration" and "migration," is used here to attempt to retain some of the complexity and consequences of definitions, as well as the relations between categories of refugees, migrants, and immigrants. According to Anna Kuroczycka Schultes and Helen Vallianatos, refugees are frequently viewed as being subject to state violence or persecution, while migrants may be moving in order to improve their prospects for their families (2016, 1–2). While not all migrants become immigrants, most immigrants have at one time or another been migrants, in the broadest sense, even if they have not been refugees.[3] The category of im/migrant literature rests problematically but inevitably on authorship, with im/migrant literature being written by im/migrants or their descendants. Wolfgang Behschnitt uses the term "migrant literature" to discuss fiction in Sweden. He also discusses problems of definition and classification, but demonstrates that this category circulates in Swedish literary discourse and literary practice, and that authors themselves "take part in public debate and inscribe themselves into the discourse on literature, migration and cultural diversity" (2010, 81).

Sweden is today known for an immigration and refugee policy which has made it one of the leading European nations for immigration in twenty-first-century Europe, and these demographic trends, as Anna Williams notes, have come to influence contemporary literature, where im/migration and its many consequences have become a strong theme, frequently in work by children of first-generation immigrants (2021, 122). Sweden's modern immigration history begins, however, toward the end of World War II when it began to accept refugees from the war, even if Jewish people were not considered to be political refugees at the time, but were considered by the Swedish authorities as immigrants (Kvist Geverts 2020,

---

[3] The 1951 Refugee Convention defines refugees as being outside their country of nationality due to persecution or fear of persecution on multiple grounds, and the United Nations High Commissioner for Refugees has since expanded this definition. See, for example, the UNHCR website.

154).[4] In spite of the long-standing presence of Jews in Sweden, Scandinavian Jews fleeing persecution were first admitted in 1943 and European Jews in 1944 (Grobgeld and Bursell 2021, 175). Other European Jews were taken in on at least a provisional basis from 1944, as the war neared its end. About 4000 of those Jewish immigrants who came stayed in Sweden after the war, as did Silberstein's mother and, eventually, her father. This makes Silberstein one of the estimated 20,000 Jewish persons living in Sweden today, where Jews are a recognized national minority. In today's Sweden, where 20% of the population is foreign-born, she is also among the 5% of the population born in Sweden to two foreign-born parents (Grobgeld and Bursell 2021, 175–176).

Though it seems obvious that Holocaust survivors have been both refugees and im/migrants to new countries, im/migrant status has been somewhat submerged in accounts by children of survivors, who instead view the Holocaust as the defining experience of their parents' and not infrequently their own lives. *Förintelsens Barn*, I suggest, engages with cultural narratives of both postmemory and im/migrant identity, both of which influence the representation of motherhood and the figure of the mother. Silberstein's mother is represented as resilient and tenacious, but also as "broken" (134), a woman who survives the horrors of the camps but fails to rid herself of the trauma or to completely assimilate to Swedish society. In keeping with both narratives, the daughter's view of the mother and motherhood in this postmemorial account is marked by strong ambivalence.

## POSTMEMORY AS A GENERATIONAL CONCERN

From the 1980s onward, in Sweden as well as in other countries to which survivors settled after the war, autobiographies and family memoirs written by children of survivors began to explore what it meant to grow up in families marked by a history of genocide.[5] While the experiences them-

---

[4] See Kvist Geverts (2020) for a discussion of discriminatory processing of Jewish immigration applications between 1938 and 1944, as well as for controversies around Swedish wartime treatment of Jews.

[5] English-language texts such as Art Spiegelman's graphic memoir *Maus* (1996) or Anne Karpf's *The War After* (1996), like Swedish-language texts such as Susanne Levin's *Leva Vidare* (1994), emerged in contexts of Holocaust denial and the loss of survivors, generating critical thought on issues such as the legacy of the Holocaust and the intergenerational transmission of trauma and memory.

selves undoubtedly contribute to a sense of group identity, the sharing of childhood memories and narrativization of post-Holocaust family life have become fundamental to the generational distinctiveness of the generation known as the postmemory generation. Coined by another child of survivors, Marianne Hirsch (2012), "postmemory" refers not to an actual individual memory but to the forceful, affective traces of someone else's—usually a survivor parent's—memory of traumatic experiences as these traces are apprehended by their children. Hirsch's formulations have been foundational in academic discourses on the Holocaust, trauma, and memory, and thus, they, too, contribute to a sense of generational distinctiveness. Investigating survivors, rather than children of survivors, Rebecca Clifford's conclusions about generational identity are nevertheless relevant: "While formative events are important, a shared process of remembering and narrating is more so, fired into action by a historical context that can emerge decades after the fact" (2017, 23). In line with this insight, this chapter views *Förintelsens Barn* as joining an established narrative and discursive tradition which foregrounds family trauma, parental transmission, and child susceptibility. Publishing later than many of the first children of survivors, Silberstein both assumes and explores the idea that her parents' Holocaust experiences have a bearing on her childhood, her adult relationship with her mother, and her own practice of mothering, to which her two adult sons testify in the final chapters of her book.

To consider Silberstein's text as part of an established narrative and discursive tradition is certainly not intended to discount the reality or validity of her account. Instead, it is meant to acknowledge the ways that such traditions may affect the formation and understanding of identity, and the way that they can contribute to other cultural narratives of, for example, post-Holocaust family and motherhood.[6] While postmemorial life writing offers loving and positive portraits of survivor motherhood, many accounts by children of survivors also present complex and fraught relations. Hirsch elaborates on the consequences of postmemory for children of survivors:

> To grow up with overwhelming inherited memories, to be dominated by narratives that preceded one's birth or one's consciousness, is to risk having

---

[6] In Holocaust witness studies, considerable attention has been given to the way that interview protocols, narrative, and media use can shape testimony. See, for example, Shenker (2015).

one's own life stories displaced, even evacuated, by our ancestors. It is to be shaped, however indirectly, by traumatic fragments of events that still defy narrative reconstruction and exceed comprehension. These events happened in the past, but their effects continue into the present. (2012, 5)

Together with trauma and memory studies, works of autobiography and memoir thus also contribute to a widespread assumption of problematic or pathological parenting among survivors.[7] As one sociologist summarizes it, there is an "overwhelming impression that trauma is the central if not dominant dynamic in the family lives and memories of [children of survivors]" (Wolf 2019, 74). Thus, the intergenerational transmission of trauma remains key to the now classic understanding of children of survivors as the postmemory generation, arguably also affecting how these children—now parents and even grandparents themselves—understand themselves, their families, and their mothers.

This chapter argues that *Förintelsens Barn* largely conforms to the postmemory narrative in its treatment of maternal identity and transmission of Holocaust trauma. At the same time, the text overlaps with the emerging genre of im/migrant autobiography in Sweden—a genre which also has generational concerns at its heart. These two narratives affect the author's portrayal and understanding of mothering and motherhood—of both Ili and of Margit—after the Holocaust and in Sweden. In other words, while complex mother-daughter relations are important to Silberstein's interrogation of the legacy of the Holocaust and the transmission of memory, *Förintelsens Barn* moves toward an overlapping definition of itself as immigrant or minority autobiography.

## HOLOCAUST MOTHERS AND DAUGHTERS

In a significant number of English-language postmemory narratives by children of survivors from about the 1980s onward, second-generation daughters take pains to represent their mother's voices. Hybrid texts frequently result from the inclusion of quotations or entire sections from interviews or written accounts. In this way, postmemorial writing at least

---

[7]The intergenerational transmission of trauma continues to be investigated in psychology and medicine. See Payne and Berle, 2020, for a recent overview. See also Wolf, 2019, for a discussion of recent trends toward documenting the transmission of resilience and joy among survivors.

partially offsets the literary dominance of the daughter's voice over that of the mother. Postmemory writing in Swedish also has examples of this effort to include the maternal voice. In Susanne Levin's *Leva vidare* (1994, *Live on*), Anders Ohlsson observes (2000, 31–33), the third-person narrative focalizes the mother, and Lena Einhorn's *Ninas resa* (2005) incorporates her mother's words, recorded in interviews with her daughter, in both text and film versions. *Förintelsens Barn* both conforms to and deviates from this pattern. The work does contain sparse excerpts from letters written by Silberstein's father to her mother after the war, as he waited to immigrate to Sweden. Silberstein and her brother did not have these letters translated from the Hungarian so they could read them until after the deaths of both parents, however. Her mother's letters to her father, if any existed, were not preserved. Nor is there any indication that Silberstein used her journalistic skills to interview her mother about her Holocaust experiences. The daughter's perspective is dominant in *Förintelsens Barn*, though motherhood is central to the narrative.

Silberstein's text conceives of motherhood much as Adrienne Rich (1995, 13) would have it, as a position and an identity which is culturally, socially, and historically constructed. The very premise of the narrative, evident from the epigraph to this chapter, implicitly endorses the view that Holocaust history has had a strong effect on family life and Ili's practice of mothering. Silberstein's narrative undertaking is to explain what the Holocaust "did" to her parents and her family and to connect this to generational transmission within families, to the idea that the Holocaust also did something to her and her brother, and ultimately to Silberstein's own children. The view of historically contingent mothering also emerges explicitly in her explanations of specific practices common to Holocaust survivors, such as her mother's choice to name Margit after her favorite sister, murdered by the Nazis (24–25), and her mother's encouragement of family solidarity (111). Additionally, Silberstein poses the related question of whether Holocaust survival affected the practice of parenthood in her family: "What parents would Mother and Father have been if there had not been an Auschwitz? This is impossible to answer. So that which was difficult for my brother and me in our relationship to mom and dad we usually attributed to the Holocaust" (113).[8] Silberstein observes a pro-

---

[8] "Vilka föräldrar hade mamma och pappa varit om inte Auschwitz funnits? Det går inte att svara på. Så det som var svårt för min bror och mig i vår relation till mamma och pappa tillskrev vi oftast Förintelsen" (113).

pensity to explain relational difficulties, "that which was difficult," as an effect of Holocaust experience.

But what *was* difficult in the mother-daughter relationship, which Silberstein attributes to Ili's Holocaust experiences? Her mother's strongest convictions about the meaning of life, according to Silberstein, grew out of her survival of the camps: "Mother's answer to the question of how a life after Auschwitz was possible is one word: the children. To have a new family" (57).[9] Ili's assertion resonates with the sentiments of numerous survivors and their descendants, (including Silberstein later in life), in which the post-Holocaust creation of Jewish family successfully rebukes and defies the Nazis' genocidal ambitions (Grobgeld and Bursell 2021, 178). For the child Margit, however, having such importance to the lives and happiness of one's parents was a heavy burden. Silberstein writes, "My brother and I became their salvation, we gave them meaning and they loved us more than anything else on this earth. Is all-encompassing love only of good? It can instill self-esteem, but also consuming guilt" (27). She reflects as well on what she felt was the disproportionate significance she knew she had on her parents as a child: "One wishes to be important to one's mother and father, but maybe not everything, that is unattainable" (10). Silberstein characterizes growing up as a child of survivors as being burdened by unrealistic expectations: "I wanted to be normal, not a miracle. Not the reason for Mom and Dad to find meaning in life" (97).[10] She writes movingly, and repeatedly, of the guilt she feels in relation to her mother, both in childhood and as an adult.

Silberstein also attributes parental and maternal overprotectiveness to the profound importance placed on children in the family, who defied Hitler by their very existence, and who were also seen as symbolically replacing murdered family members, such as Silberstein's namesake, her mother's sister, or her father's little sister, Irma. As she puts it, "Holocaust survivors—they overprotect, they press their children close, they do not want to let go, they give everything and they want to get in return, unconditional love …" (113). Both parents watched over her health, for nothing

---

[9] "Mammas svar på frågan om hur ett liv efter Auschwitz var möjligt är ett ord: barnen. Att få en ny familj" (57).
[10] "Jag och min bror blev deras räddning, vi gav dem mening och de älskade oss över allt annat på denna jord. Är allomfattande kärlek enbart av godo? Den kan ge självkänsla, men också förtärande skuld" (27); "Man vill såklart vara betydelsefull för sin mor och far, men kanske inte allt, det är ouppnåeligt" (10); "Jag ville vara vanlig, inte något underverk. Inte anledningen till att mamma och pappa kunde finna mening i livet" (97).

was to happen to their little family (42). She tells of a playmate who was also a child of survivors who thought her name was "Barbro-be-careful," because that was what her mother called to her as she supervised her play from the window of their home. Silberstein claims that she became a "Margit-be-careful" because "Nothing was to happen to me. I was to always be strong and healthy, happy and good" (43). Being overprotected, moreover, is connected in the text to unreasonable expectations, such as always being good and nice: "If you are a child of Holocaust survivors you must always be nice—that's how it felt. I could have a guilty conscience if I went home with my best friend after school ... instead of asking Mother if she needed help with anything. All my pores were wide open for self-recriminations" (98).[11] Silberstein's adult understanding of maternal (over)protectiveness conforms to that expressed in numerous other post-memory narratives, and examples abound in *Förintelsens Barn*.

Silberstein writes about both of her parents and describes her father in loving terms, but her mother is clearly central to the household and to Silberstein as a child. Numerous interviews with the author confirm her mother's importance: "Mother was central in our family" (Cederskog 2021); " there was a lot of Mamma"; "Mamma was a strong person in our lives" (Silberstein 2021b). [12] As a child, Silberstein is very close to her mother, whom she resembles (23). A skilled seamstress and embroiderer whose talents were sought after in their small town, Ili hated being alone (47) and liked to talk with her daughter as she sewed (44). Unlike Silberstein's father, who never spoke about what happened in the Soviet labor camp, Ili spoke of her life before and during the war, communicating her experiences to her young daughter, both through storytelling and through less verbal means, in line with Federica K. Clementi's suggestion, in *Holocaust Mothers and Daughters* (2013), that mothers seem to share their memories with their children, more than fathers do (218). In one interview, Silberstein claims that "What I know I know through Mother,"

---

[11] "Om man är barn till överlevande från Förintelsen måste man alltid vara snäll—så kändes det. Jag kunde få dåligt samvete om jag följde med min bästis hem efter skolan en stund ... istället för att fråga mamma om hon behövde hjälp med något. Alla mina porer var vidöppna för självförebråelser" (98).

[12] "Mamma var central i vår familj" (Cederskog 2021); "... det har varit väldigt mycket mamma" och "Mamma var en stark person i våran liv" (Silberstein 2021b). In this interview Silberstein says that her mother spoke from endless grief, but she did not give any details. "The camp" functioned as a code word in the family.

even though she says that her mother did not give any details about her Holocaust experiences (Silberstein 2021b).[13]
In *Förintelsens Barn* Silberstein observes:

> I was born five years after the liberation of Auschwitz and Bergen-Belsen and when Mother talked to me when I was a child her entire consciousness was filled with the horrors and the bottomless loss of those who died. Somehow, I became a confidante. I know, psychologists would be horrified. She absolutely did not tell me everything, but a lot. My imagination filled the gaps with grotesque, dark imaginings, thoughts that a child should not need to be caught up in. (44–45)[14]

Registering her adult awareness of the negative view psychology would take of her mother making her child a confidante, Silberstein subtly criticizes her mother. She also reflects on the reasons for her mother's confidences: Ili may have sought to replicate the intimacy she once had with her sister Margit. Silberstein, the postmemoirist, understands the impossibility of her child-self answering her mother's need, as well as the guilty conscience resulting from that inescapable failure (46–47).

Postmemory, as Hirsch develops the concept, involves not actual recall but is mediated by embodied affect and imagination (5). As a child, Silberstein's imagination is captured by the Holocaust, particularly camp experiences such as her mother must have undergone. For example, she writes about having "daily imaginings about selection to the gas chambers, about roll call in Auschwitz, how it was to stand completely still hour after hour in summer as well as winter, no matter the weather, before and after laboring, so that the guards could count in peace … " (95).[15] She also fantasized about accompanying her mother on the death march from

---

[13] In the television interview Silberstein (2021b) says, "Vad jag vet vet jag genom mamman." Moreover, Silberstein told her interviewer that she also absorbed that which was "unspoken" ("outtalat").

[14] "Jag föddes fem år efter befrielsen av Auschwitz och Bergen-Belsen och när mamma pratade med mig som liten var hela hennes medvetande fyllt av fasorna och den bottenlösa saknaden efter de döda. På något sätt blev jag en förtrogen. Jag vet, psykologer skulle förfäras. Hon berättade absolut inte allt, men åtskilligt. Luckorna fyllde fantasin i med groteska, mörka föreställningar, tankar som ett barn inte ska behöva svepas in i" (44–45).

[15] "Jag kunde ha dagliga föreställningar om selekteringen till gaskamrarna, om appellerna i Auschwitz, hur det var att stå helt stilla timme efter timme sommar som vinter, oavsett vädret, före och efter arbetet, för att vakterna i lugn och ro skulle kunna räkna så att antalet fångar stämde" (95).

Auschwitz to Bergen-Belsen, and reading books such as *Barnen från Frostmofjället* about orphaned brothers and sisters setting out on a long trek to avoid being put into a poorhouse (85) fed this imaginative connection to her mother. As Hirsch notes, even intimate transmission of memories in the domestic or familial context are mediated by public narratives (35). Claiming that she cannot remember a time when she did not know what Auschwitz was (43), Silberstein also describes being strongly drawn to pain: "I wanted to go into it, feel it, let the intolerable, the incomprehensible, burn in me as well. As if my mother's torture could be lessened if I shared it with her" (83).[16] This form of imaginative identification, strong in a child who idolizes her mother (100), leads the young Silberstein to reproduce her mother's physical suffering in a vain attempt to alleviate it. She stops eating: "I starved myself so that only a thin skin covered my skeleton. Did I want to be as thin as mother in Auschwitz?" (83).

In her study of Holocaust mothers and daughters, Clementi analyzes another postmemoir which, like *Förintelsens Barn*, suggests that "eating disorders [are] displaced symptoms of traumatic Shoah memory or postmemory" (2013, 206).[17] In Silberstein's case, her anorexia does indeed suggest a "dislocation" of daughterly identity (Clementi 2013, 206), a misplaced identification with her mother through self-harm. Far from alleviating her mother's burden, Silberstein only exacerbates Ili's pain at seeing her daughter starve as she, her sisters, and others in the camps once did. At one point, Ili tells her daughter that her emaciated body is a reminder to her, and others, of the horrors of Bergen-Belsen (85).

Silberstein appears to have viewed her parents as vulnerable and fragile, because of the suffering, starvation, and illnesses they had been through, only some of which she knew about. She writes that she later understood that many survivors "suffered from the same syndrome as my mother.

[16] "När jag var barn hade smärtan en nästan befängd dragningskraft på mig. Jag ville gå in i den, känna den, låta det outhärdliga, det ofattbara, brinna också i mig. Som om mon mors plågor skulle mildras om jag delade dem med henne."

[17] Clementi writes about Helena Janeczek's *Lezioni di tenebra* (1997). Irene Oore's *The Listener* (2019) recounts Holocaust episodes of extreme hunger as well as the daughter Oore's remarkable suggestion to her survivor mother, late in life, that she stops eating in order to avoid choking. Anca Vlasopolos's *No Return Address* (2000) also concerns questions of food.

Depression, nightmares, nervosity, sleep disturbances" (99).[18] Her reference to a "syndrome" confirms her familiarity with works of memoir and postmemoir, and this is underscored by the text's many references to Holocaust writers such as Primo Levi, Elie Wiesel, Charlotte Delbo, and Anne Frank: Frank's diary was particularly important to the young Silberstein, who thought that if Frank had lived they would have been "twin souls" (88). Frank's writing may even have inspired Silberstein to keep the diary from which she quotes in her autobiography.

As in other works of postmemory, *Förintelsens Barn* represents the daughter's attempt to imitate or emulate her mother as futile:

> But my torture could never measure up to hers. I did not have much of a claim, it was always worse for mother. How sad could I permit myself to be? My troubles were small and not very significant, silly, compared with that which mother bore, what did I have to complain about? Mother of course did not want me to feel that way, I am not even sure if she understood how her daughter was influenced by what she herself went through. (83–84).[19]

Silberstein repeatedly confirms the fraught sentiments of postmemory—a sense of being dominated by other's narratives, of having one's own story displaced by another's traumatic history. In Silberstein's text, this appears to be particularly strong between her and her survivor mother.

## IM/MIGRANT MOTHERS AND MINORITY DAUGHTERS

This chapter has thus far focused on Silberstein's representation of the effect of Holocaust survival on her mother, the mother-daughter bond, and her mother's mothering practices. This representation is for the most part in line with other postmemorial accounts by children of survivors. But postmemory writing itself also encompasses, to varying degrees, representations of survivor parents and their families as im/migrants to new

[18] "Jag förstod senare att många, antagligen de flesta, som kommit levande ut från fasor som inte går att sätta ord på, led av samma syndrom som min mamma. Nedstämdhet, mardrömmar, nervositet, sömnproblem" (99).

[19] "Jag svalt mig själv så att bara tunt skinn skylde skelettet. Ville jag bli lika mager som mamma i Auschwitz? Men mina plågor kunde aldrig mäta sig med hennes. Jag hade inte mycket att komma med, det var alltid värst för mamma. Hur ledsen kunde jag tillåta mig att vara? Mina bekymmer var små och inte så betydelsefulla, futtiga, jämfört med det mamma bar på, vad hade jag att klaga över? Mamma ville förstås inte att jag skulle känna så, jag vet inte ens om hon förstod hur hennes dotter påverkades av det hon själv gått igenom" (83–84).

countries. Hirsch emphasizes that the postmemory generation is always in some respect diasporic, marginal, or exiled (qtd in Clementi 2013, 221), and Clementi concurs. She writes:

> On the one hand, all survivors want is for their children to be happy, safe, and prosperous in the free society where they have rebuilt their lives; on the other, because the parents themselves strain to fully belong to these new nations—where they arrived as adults with a heavy burden of pain and with accents, traditions, and social behaviors they retain—their children like them may end up feeling split between fully belonging ... and being foreigners in their country of birth (Clementi 2013, 219).

In *Förintelsens Barn*, im/migration exists as an alternative explanation for Ili's mothering practices, affecting her relationship with her daughter and her daughter's understanding of her own and her mother's identity. Silberstein quite explicitly inserts her writing into a discourse of im/migration and minority identity in contemporary Sweden.

Silberstein relates her mother's story of post-war im/migration with pride. Her mother arrived from Bergen-Belsen to Norrköping on July 8, 1945. Twenty-eight years old, weighing just thirty-four kilos, Ili was transported on a stretcher (51). She lived at first with other im/migrants in a repurposed school, where she was nursed back to health (58), and later she rented a room, made friends, and began working at the public bathhouse (59). Among the letters from Silberstein's father is one deploring the fact that Ili must work for a living. Yet, Silberstein appears proud of her mother when she writes, "My mother was not lazy. She was clever and industrious. She personified the expression, 'someone who earns her keep'" (59).[20] In Transylvania, she had had to give up her dream of becoming a teacher for financial reasons, and she had instead learned to machine embroider, like other Romanian girls. In Norrköping, Ili starts up a cottage industry in their small apartment, embroidering sheets and towels and other dowry items. Silberstein proudly quotes from the royal permit allowing Ili to run her embroidery business as long as she remained in Norrköping, even though she was not a Swedish citizen (60). After Silberstein's father arrived, the two of them cooperated in the business which, in the 1950s, fit nicely into the town's burgeoning textile industry.

---

[20] "Min mamma latade sig inte. Hon var duktig och arbetsam. Hon personifierar uttrycket, 'en som gör rätt för sig'" (59). The expression has additional connotations, including doing one's part and doing right by others.

Her parents learned Swedish, her mother better than her father (71), but they often spoke Hungarian to one another, sometimes, to their daughter's embarrassment, in public (31). Her father worked at the wool textile factory and later at another factory for electronics, but in the 1960s he and Ili opened a shoe store together. Both parents are represented as working hard, for long hours, to support themselves and their two children, building a new life in a new country which had taken them in after the war (31).

Silberstein's childhood memories offer a view of the economic hardships common to refugees or im/migrants who have had to start their lives over from scratch, but who are successful in supporting themselves and their children, even buying luxury items such as a piano for their child. Her memories, frequently nostalgic, recount both what they could afford and what they could not (110). Highly attuned to the nuances of class society in the 1950s, Silberstein describes her family's small apartment with cold water and a shared bathroom in the courtyard, contrasting it with that of her friend, who shared an indoor bathroom, and with the street where some of her classmates lived, in apartments large enough that children could have their own rooms. On this street, the children addressed their parents with formality (28). Silberstein recounts an incident from her childhood, when her family's economic status made itself felt. She enjoyed talking to the women who contracted sewing from her mother so much that when they came round to leave or pick up work from Ili, the young Silberstein routinely offered them coffee so they would stay. Her tired mother finally had to ask her not to prolong these visits, which kept her from her work. Silberstein's awareness of economic status is something she seemed to process by playing what she called "The Poverty Game" (86) as a child—a game of endless wandering inspired by her mother's camp experiences and by a classic of Swedish children's literature involving orphaned children, *Barnen från Frostmofjället*. But in other ways she appears to be unaware of economic difficulties; only in hindsight does she register the sacrifices her parents must have made to give their daughter a piano, and she does not take in the financial side of her and her brother being sent to camp in the US. Silberstein's postmemoir contains traces of what must have been difficult parental decisions.

As Schultes and Vallianatos observe, im/migrants are frequently confronted with a choice between enacting mothering practices based on their own experiences in the culture of their birth and their sometimes incomplete understanding of practices common to their new country (3). By extension, parenting practices thus become an index of the degree of

social integration and/or im/migrant difference. These different orientations in the performance of parenthood are made visible in Silberstein's
text. Her father grew up in rural Romania where, before the war, a strict
morality governed relations between boys and girls (72).[21] Her mother
came from Satu Mare, a county seat in Transylvania with a thriving Jewish
community. Silberstein's parents wanted to parent in ways they knew from
before the war. Their rules were strict, and Margit was not allowed to be
out late or to do everything that her friends were allowed to do. Both
parents, she writes, feared an all-too liberal Swedish behavior (71). Neither
parent could accept "that their daughter was stamped by Swedish society,
entirely different from the society they had been forced to leave, a world
which in their memory had come to a standstill, like a snapshot in a photo
album" (133).[22] In other words, according to Silberstein, both parents
performed at least some aspects of parenthood in opposition to what they
understood about Swedish practices.

Generational conflicts between parents and daughter were exacerbated
by cultural differences around issues of parental supervision and the independence of young people. Silberstein describes her teenage years as a
time of growing estrangement from her mother in particular, whose "children lived in a world which she could not enter, which she did not want
to enter" (136).[23] Silberstein's anorexia, as mentioned, indicates the inten-
sity with which she identifies with her mother at this time, but her retrospective account also emphasizes her growing need for personal integrity.
As she puts it, "It was not even that Mother and Father wanted to cross
boundaries, my boundaries, they saw none. We were family, a constellation
without barriers ..." (134).[24] Silberstein describes trying to explain to her
mother that "children must cut the umbilical cord, free themselves, learn
to fly. No one owns another person, not even parents in relation to their
offspring. She really did not understand, she became sad, she thought this

---

[21] Much of Transylvania changed hands between Hungary and Romania in 1920 and then
before and after the World War II.
[22] "Mamma och pappa förmådde inte acceptera att deras dotter präglats av den svenska
samhället, helt annorlunda än det de tvingats lämna, en värld som i deras minne stannat upp,
som en ögonblicksbild i ett fotoalbum" (133).
[23] "Hennes barn levde i en värld dit hon inte hade tillträde, hon ville inte komma in" (136).
[24] "Det var inte ens så att mamma och pappa ville överträda gränser, mina gränser, de såg
inga. Vi var familj, en konstellation utan barriärer ..." (134).

meant that I would disappear from her, leave her" (130–31).[25] When Silberstein does in fact leave home, she experiences a crisis of identity, not understanding her own boundaries in relation to her parents (133). While Silberstein clearly attributes the importance of family to her mother's Holocaust experience, as discussed, there remain elements which can be linked to the experience of im/migrant motherhood, with Ili drawing from her experiences of Jewish family life in pre-war Romania, and her daughter rooted firmly in the modern social welfare state of Sweden. Silberstein describes clashes with her parents over issues such as privacy and openness, independence and mutuality, and not least, sexuality.

While mothers have been found to have a strong influence on their daughters' identity formation and sexuality (Giorgio 2002, 7), such a relation—anticipated by Ili, we can surmise—appears to be disrupted by the different orientations of mother and daughter, one more affected by her im/migrant status, the other by her "native" status. The estrangement between mother and daughter worsens as Silberstein's sexuality awakens, and mild conflicts escalate when Silberstein becomes sexually active: "When Mother understood that her adult daughter had adult relations she lost her grip. I felt like all hell broke loose, she plagued me, she said things that a mother should never say to her little girl" (135).[26] The text remains reticent about what harsh words were spoken, and the timeline of sections dealing with these issues is fuzzy, but there appears to be a breach in the mother-daughter relationship which is never to be completely overcome.

Silberstein's survivor parents were not just invested in their family but were also strongly invested in the reproduction and continuity of family. In part because of matrilineal descent in Judaism, their daughter is important. Silberstein recalls the period after she moved away from home, when her non-Jewish boyfriend lived with her on weekends. Silberstein feels responsible for her mother having a heart attack during this time: "I was not like they wanted me to be, I lived like 'the Swedes.' I had the key to their happiness, but I threw it away. If I only would marry and let them experience the joy of grandchildren their lives would change, they would

---

[25] "En gång försökte jag förklara för mamma att barn måste klippa navelsträngen, lösgöra sig, flyga själva. Ingen äger en annan människa, inte ens föräldrar i förhållande till avkomman. Hon förstod verkligen//inte, hon blev ledsen, hon uppfattade det som att jag skulle försvinna från henne, lämna henne" (130–31).

[26] "När mamma förstod att hennes vuxna dotter hade vuxna relationer förlorade hon fotfästet. Jag kände det som att helvetet bröt lös, hon plågade mig, hon sa saker som en mamma inte ska säga till sin flicka" (135).

become happy" (135).[27] While the desire for descendants can certainly be understood as springing from a history of survival in the face of ethnic persecution, the anticipated parental supervision of reproduction within the family is represented as also grounded in pre-war Jewish life in Romania.

As a child of im/migrant survivor parents, Silberstein struggles with conflicting understandings of herself as the child of survivors, as a member of the Jewish minority, and as a Swede. There is considerable overlap between these categories and the first two, if not identical, are strongly related in Silberstein's mind. During a trip to Romania after her mother's death, she realizes, to her distress, that she feels her mother most strongly in Auschwitz, suggesting the strength of the association between her mother and the Holocaust as well as the weight of the Holocaust on her own sense of Jewishness. In conversation with her adult sons, she sees that the Holocaust is intrinsic to her Jewish identity (181). Silberstein also conceptualizes her bi-cultural or dual identity with the help of her "Jewish" name and her "Swedish" name, a Jewish identity strongly connected to the Holocaust through her mother's murdered sister, Margit, and a Swedish identity forged from her parents' mistaken belief that Asta was a typically Swedish name (24). Her parents' choice of names clearly speaks of their early recognition that their daughter will need to negotiate the demands of being both Swedish and Jewish.

Silberstein's narrative inscribes a struggle to harmonize dual identities, both as a young person and as a mother herself. Indeed, she expresses the desire that her twin sons will also have a dual identity, as Swedes and Jews (174). While, as noted, there is no trace of interviews or other records of Ili's voice in *Förintelsens Barn*, Silberstein does interview her twin sons, Markus and Joel, reporting their thoughts using indirect discourse in the penultimate chapter of her book. Her interest is in understanding what their Jewish background means to them, but also in determining if she, through her mothering, has unwillingly transmitted to them the trauma of the Holocaust. Silberstein reviews her maternal ambitions, frequently in relation to her own mother's practices. Since she grew up feeling diffuse but debilitating guilt in relation to her mother and the Holocaust, she tried hard to avoid giving her children any feelings of guilt (174). Because

---

[27] "Jag var inte som de ville, jag levde som 'svenskarna'. Jag hade nyckeln till deras lycka, men jag slängde den i sjön. Om jag bara gifte mig och lät dem uppleva lyckan i att få barn-barn skulle deras liv förändras, de skulle bli lyckliga" (135).

she listened to the warning of the little girl "who sat at a small red table next to her machine-embroidering mother and listened to stories about Auschwitz" (175), she tried not to talk too much about the Holocaust when her boys were small. She sought to encourage and protect their integrity. The responses of her children suggest that, in spite of her strenuous efforts, she did transmit strong emotions about the Holocaust. One son felt the weight of her unspoken sorrow and instinctively encouraged her to express her grief. Her other son expresses the same feeling she had as a child, that he seemed always to have known about the Holocaust, and he remembers her as talking about it even before he began to wonder about it, though she chose her words carefully (176). Both sons see her as an overprotective mother, and one reflects on the psychological and emotional burden her strong concern for them generates. Silberstein explains: "That I am so caring about him and his brother, so afraid of instilling a guilty conscience because I have lived with one myself, also creates some type of guilt feeling in him" (184). Yet, her sons also affirm, in different ways, a commitment to Jewish identity and the remembrance of Holocaust history. Silberstein's interviews with her adult sons return her readers to the narrative of postmemory, exploring the intergenerational transmission of Holocaust memory to the third generation and confirming the continued relevance of Jewish identity in a Swedish context.

*Förintelsens Barn* writes itself into discourses of both postmemory and im/migration. Im/migration concerns not only Silberstein's survivor parents, their Romanian Jewish roots, and their im/migration to Sweden, but Silberstein herself as a Swedish Jew conceived explicitly and increasingly as the text progresses as a minority: "I am Swedish. A Swedish Jew. A Jew in Sweden. A person who belongs to another religion than the majority and to a partly different culture" (161).[28] She writes to provide insights into what it means to belong to a minority in Sweden (188) and sees the struggle to maintain two identities as common among young people "who are tossed around in a centrifuge between two worlds and don't know where or how to land" (136).[29] She suggests that "Maybe young people with roots in other countries can recognize my experiences. To belong, but also

---

[28] "Jag är svensk. Svensk judinna. En judinna i Sverige. En människa som tillhör en annan religion än majoriteten och delvis en annan kultur" (161).
[29] "som slungas runt i en centrifug mellan två världar och inte vet var och hur de ska landa" (136).

to have another belonging" (189).[30] With her explicit focus on young people, reinforced by the dedication of her book to her sons Markus and Joel, Silberstein positions herself as a maternal, minority figure, who was once a daughter to im/migrant parents. She concludes with the hope that her story might help young immigrants know that they are not alone (189).

## Conclusion

The notion of intergenerational transmission of traumatic memory through mother-child interaction—both backward and forward in time— is integral to Silberstein's work. *Förintelsens Barn* captures the importance of the survivor mother to the daughter's sense of self, and it examines the effects of the Holocaust on the performance of motherhood, as seen in the maternal practices of her mother and later of herself, to which her sons testify in the final chapters of the book. Silberstein displays a keen awareness of the narrative parameters of postmemory writing, and she clearly inserts her text into this tradition, to which parent-child relations are central.

While complex mother-daughter relations are important to Silberstein's interrogation of the legacy of the Holocaust and the transmission of memory, *Förintelsens Barn* simultaneously moves to define itself as im/migrant or minority literature. In part, Silberstein accomplishes this by representing her parents as im/migrants as much as survivors, facing many of the challenges common to refugees and im/migrants, including learning a new language, making a living through hard work, and raising children in an unfamiliar climate. Her mother's mothering practices and attitudes toward her daughter, she suggests, are as strongly influenced by her im/migrant status as by her Holocaust experience. But Silberstein also inserts her writing into the category of im/migrant writing by representing herself as having a dual identity, one of which is as a minority.

Clifford argues that "Members of a self-defined generation must have a subjective sense of collective belonging, and the work of forging this generational identity is itself deeply shaped by its own historical moment" (2017, 23). Silberstein publishes her work at a time of tension concerning im/migration to Sweden. Because of instability in the Middle East, increasing numbers of people from Iran, Iraq, Syria, and Afghanistan have

---

[30] "Kanske känner unga människor med rötter i andra länder igen sig i mina upplevelser. Detta att tillhöra, men att också ha en annan tillhörighet" (189).

sought refuge in Sweden. Im/migrants with Muslim background have become significant in number. At the same time, the Sweden Democrats, a conservative, nationalist anti-immigration political party, have gained parliamentary representation and as of 2022 collaborate with the Swedish government. Antisemitism in Sweden has been reported to be on the rise, in a variety of contexts, even if there also appears to be a general weakening of support for antisemitic opinions in Sweden (Brå 2019, 7–9; Bachner and Bevelander, 2021).This social context, as well as the historical context of the Holocaust, appears to shape Silberstein's understanding of audience and purpose, as well as her dual sense of self. She articulates a sense of what has been termed the multidirectionality of Holocaust memory, the idea that collective memories of different groups take shape via a dynamic, intercultural process in a landscape of memory traditions vying for attention and recognition, and that knowledge and insight can be gained from exchanges between the Holocaust and other memory traditions (Rothberg 2009, 21). In other words, looking both forward and backward from the entwined positions of daughter and mother, Silberstein brings Holocaust postmemoir into dialogue with im/migrant autobiography, establishing some common ground with im/migrants and their descendants in Sweden today.[31]

REFERENCES

Bachner, Henrik, and Pieter Bevelander. 2021. *Antisemitism i Sverige: En jäm-förelse av attityder och föreställningar 2005 och 2020*. Stockholm: Forum för Levande Historia.

Behschnitt, Wolfgang. 2010. The Voice of the 'Real Migrant': Contemporary Migration Literature in Sweden. In *Migration and Literature in Contemporary Europe*, ed. Mirjam Gebauer and Pia Schwarz Lausten, 77–92. Munich: Martin Meidenbauer.

Brå (Brottsförebyggande Rådet/The Swedish National Council for Crime Prevention). 2019. *Antisemitiska hatbrott*. Report no. 4. Stockholm: Brottsförebyggande rådet. https://bra.se/download/18.62c6cfa2166eca 5d70e19304/1615395061042/2019_4_Antisemitiska_hatbrott.pdf

Cederskog, George. 2021. Margit Silberstein: Mina föräldrars ryggsäckar blev också min tyngd *Dagens Nyheter*, 10 January.

---

[31] This work was supported by the Foundation for Baltic and East European Studies under Grant number 1364/3.1.1/2015.

Clementi, Frederica K. 2013. *Holocaust Mothers and Daughters: Family, History and Trauma*. Waltham, MA: Brandeis UP.

Clifford, Rebecca. 2017. Who is a Survivor? Child Holocaust Survivors and the Development of a Generational Identity. *Oral History/ Forum d'historie orale* 37, 1-23.

Giorgio, Adalgisa. 2002. Introduction: Mothers and Daughters in Western Europe: Mapping the Territory. In *Writing Mothers and Daughters: Renegotiating the Mother in Western European Narratives by Women*, ed. Adalgisa Giorgio, 1–10. New York: Berhahn Books.

Grobgeld, David, and Moa Bursell. 2021. Resisting Assimilation: Ethnic Boundary Maintenance among Jews in Sweden. *Distinktion: Journal of Social Theory* 22 (2): 171–191. https://doi.org/10.1080/1600910X.2021.1885460.

Hirsch, Marianne. 2012. *The Generation of Postmemory: Writing and Visual Culture After the Holocaust*. New York: Columbia UP.

Kvist Geverts, Karin. 2020. Refugee Policy in Sweden during the Holocaust. A Historiographical Overview. *Holocaust Remembrance and Representation: Documentation from a Research Conference*, 143–161. Stockholm: SOU.

Kvist Geverts, Karin. 2021. Tracing the Holocaust in Early Writings in Post-War Sweden. In *Early Holocaust Memory in Sweden: Archives, Testimonies and Reflections*, ed. Johannes Heuman and Pontus Rudberg, 139–161. Cham, Switzerland: Palgrave Macmillan.

Kuroczycka Schultes, Anna, and Helen Vallianatos. 2016. Introduction: The Migrant Maternal. In *The Migrant Maternal: 'Birthing' New Lives Abroad*, ed. Anna Kuroczycka Schultes and Helen Vallianatos, 1–15. Bradford, ON: Demeter P.

Ohlsson, Anders. 2000. Förintelselitteraturen och andra generationens överlevande. *Scandinavian Jewish Studies*. 21 (1–2): 23–24.

Payne, E.A., and D. Berle. 2020. Posttraumatic Stress Disorder Symptoms Among Offspring of Holocaust Survivors: A Systematic Review and Meta-Analysis. *Traumatology* 27: 254. https://doi.org/10.1037/trm0000269.

Rich, Adrienne. 1995. *Of Woman Born: Motherhood as Experience and Institution*. New York: Norton.

Rothberg, Michael. 2009. *Multidirectional Memory: Remembering the Holocaust in the Age of Decolonization*. Stanford: Stanford UP.

Shenker, Noah. 2015. *Reframing Holocaust Testimony*. Bloomington: Indiana UP.

Silberstein, Margit. 2021a. *Förintelsens Barn*. Stockholm: Albert Bonniers förlag.

———. 2021b. "Uppväxt med Förintelsens Arv." Interview with Sharon Jåma. *SVT Nyheter*. Sveriges Television. 18 January. http://svt.se/nyheter/svtforum/forintelsens-barn-berattar

United Nations High Commission for Refugees. The 1951 Refugee Convention. Accessed 15 Feb 2022. https://www.unhcr.org/1951-refugee-convention.html.

Williams, Anna. 2021. 'My Mother Laughs, but She Never Smiles': Children, Mothers, and Migration in Contemporary Swedish Literature and Life Writing. In *Close Relations: Family, Kinship, and Beyond*, ed. Helena Wahlström Henriksson and Klara Goedecke, 121–136. Singapore: Springer.

Wolf, Diane L. 2019. Postmemories of Joy: Children of Holocaust Survivors and Alternative Family Memories. *Memory Studies* 12 (1): 74–87. https://doi.org/10.1177/1750698018811990.

# The (M)other's Voice: Representations of Motherhood in Contemporary Swiss Writing by Women

*Valerie Heffernan*

## INTRODUCTION

The late 1990s saw the emergence of a new phenomenon in German-language literature by women. Where before, translations of English, American and French novels had traditionally topped the bestseller lists in Germany, Austria and Switzerland, a new generation of writers began to make their voices heard around this time, with novels and short stories that achieved the elusive combination of both critical and commercial

This publication has received funding from the European Union's Horizon 2020 research and innovation programme under grant agreement No 952366, and from the Centre for Gender Research and the Department of Literature at Uppsala University.

V. Heffernan (✉)
School of Modern Languages, Literatures and Cultures, Maynooth University, Maynooth, Ireland
e-mail: valerie.heffernan@mu.ie

© The Author(s) 2023                                                                                          115
H. Wahlström Henriksson et al. (Eds.), *Narratives of Motherhood and Mothering in Fiction and Life Writing*, Palgrave Macmillan Studies in Family and Intimate Life,
https://doi.org/10.1007/978-3-031-17211-3_7

success. Writing in 1999, the literary critic Volker Hage drew attention to this exciting new wave of writing, enthusiastically declaring: "German literature is back in conversation and back in bookstores."[1] Interestingly, Hage asserted that this trend was led by young female writers, even going so far as to call it a literary "Fräuleinwunder"—a miracle of young ladies (Hage 1999: 245). The idea that new writing by women such as Judith Hermann, Karen Duve and Zoë Jenny was wowing readers and critics alike was not just remarkable; it was apparently downright miraculous.

Despite the condescending overtones of Hage's celebration of this new generation of authors—made all the more obvious by his use of the outdated word "Fräulein," the diminutive form of the German word "Frau," to describe these writers and their wondrous achievements—he was not the only critic to draw attention to this new development in German-language literature by women. A year earlier, Swiss literary critic Beatrice von Matt had highlighted the emergence of a new wave of female writers in German-speaking Switzerland, noting with approval, "A generation of daughters, born in the 1960s, is arriving, insolent, often witty, and self-absorbed in a rather more laid-back manner than their mothers" (Von Matt 1998a: 59). Like Hage, Von Matt noted the literary sensation that was Zoë Jenny (*1974 in Basel), and she seems to have been even more taken by Ruth Schweikert (*1965 in Lörrach). Describing Schweikert's reading of her short story "Christmas" from her collection *Erdnüsse. Totschlagen* (1994) at the annual literary festival in Solothurn—the high point of the Swiss literary calendar—she makes it clear that this was an electrifying debut. It is evident from Von Matt's remarks that she views this era as an exciting time for Swiss literature by women.[2]

Despite the interest in this wave of writing by young women sparked by Hage's and von Matt's comments (see, for example, Strigl 2001; Müller 2004; Caemmerer et al. 2005; Kocher 2005), questions remain about the extent to which their texts represent a new or innovative approach to women's writing. Does this generation of German-language writers present novel perspectives on the topics that have always preoccupied literary women? Do they offer answers to the questions raised by their literary foremothers? This chapter puts this supposedly new style of writing to the test by comparing two of the most prominent novels by Swiss women of

---

[1] "Die deutsche Literatur ist wieder im Gespräch und im Geschäft" (Hage 1999: 244).
[2] "Schaut man auf die neunziger Jahre, so fallen neue Schreibweisen auf" (Von Matt 1998b: 26).

this era—Zoë Jenny's *Das Blütenstaubzimmer* [1997, translated as *The Pollen Room*, 1998] and Ruth Schweikert's *Augen zu* [1998, untranslated]. It does so by focusing on their presentation of the mother-daughter relationship, a motif that has always played a central role in women's fiction, particularly when it has an autobiographical basis (Klages 1995, 14). It is noteworthy that both texts focus strongly on the relationship between mother and daughter and on the impact that this bond can have on the identity of both.

Taking inspiration from Marianne Hirsch's groundbreaking study *The Mother/Daughter Plot*, published less than a decade before these two novels appeared, this chapter considers the extent to which Jenny and Schweikert break with the traditional depiction of the mother-daughter relationship in literary texts. Hirsch looks back on the portrayal of mothers and daughters in literature by women from the nineteenth century right through the twentieth century. She observes that in nineteenth-century novels, such as those by Jane Austen, Mary Shelley and the Brontës, "mothers tend to be absent, silent, or devalued" (Hirsch 1989, 14). By contrast, many twentieth-century narratives by feminists such as Marguerite Duras and Margaret Atwood feature mothers prominently, but Hirsch points out that these are presented almost exclusively from the point of view of the daughter. This is, she suggests, highly problematic: "To speak for the mother [...] is at once to give voice to her discourse *and* to silence and marginalize her" (Hirsch 1989, 16). Literary texts that seek to represent women's experience of the world must, according to Hirsch, give appropriate space to maternal experience and maternal subjectivities, and it is vital that mothers have a voice in their own narratives. Hirsch thus envisions women's writing as "a feminist family romance of mothers *and* daughters, both subjects, speaking to each other and living in familial and communal contexts which enable the subjectivity of each member" (Hirsch 1989, 163, italics in original). It is in contemporary narratives by Black American women writers such as Toni Morrison and Alice Walker that Hirsch sees a way forward for women's writing. The blending of the voices of mothers and daughters that she witnesses in their work represents for Hirsch a future for women's writing: "The story of female development, both in fiction and theory, needs to be written in the voice of mothers as well as in that of daughters. [...] Only in combining both voices, in finding a double voice that would yield a multiple female consciousness, can we begin to envision ways to 'live afresh'" (Hirsch 1989, 161).

## ZOË JENNY, THE POLLEN ROOM

The Swiss writer Zoë Jenny's debut novel, *The Pollen Room*, was published in 1997 to great critical acclaim.[3] In its first year of publication, it sold over 100,000 copies in Germany and Switzerland, and it was subsequently translated into twenty-four languages. The novel won a number of prestigious literary prizes, including the 3SAT Scholarship at the Ingeborg Bachmann contest in Klagenfurt, the Literary Prize of the Jürgen Ponto Foundation, and the Aspekte Literary Prize, and critics in Switzerland and abroad hailed its author as the "voice of a whole generation" (Reinacher 1997, 89). *The Pollen Room* has been compared to other works that succeed in capturing the mood of an era, most notably to Salinger's *Catcher in the Rye* (Stocker 2002, 384). The fact that the author of this literary triumph was only twenty-three years old when it was published seems to have added to its aura, and the young, beautiful writer, who had wowed the literary critics with her candid tale, immediately enthralled the public at large. Zoë Jenny became such a celebrity in Switzerland after the appearance of *The Pollen Room* that Daniela Strigl labelled her "the press's most frequently pictured wonder-girl."[4] The success of the novel and the enormous interest in its young author even caused some critics to talk of "the phenomenon of Zoë Jenny" (Reinacher 2003, 52). Jenny herself played down her success: "I don't claim to speak for a whole generation," she says, "but I seem to have hit a nerve with some people."[5]

Jenny's novel concentrates on the plight of Jo, the child of divorced parents who is trying to find herself in the 1990s. In a sense, this is a universal tale of growing up and self-discovery, but here, it is set against a particular social backdrop—Jo's parents were children of the sixties, and Jo grew up in an atmosphere of wild parties, free love and little or no stability. In the first part of the novel, which is not quite thirteen pages long, Jo describes her childhood from the point of view of the child. Jo's parents separate shortly after she starts school, and she stays with her father, who prints books at home by day and leaves Jo alone at night to go and drive a

[3] All quotations from Zoë Jenny's novel refer to the published translation by Michael Hoffmann. All quotations from Ruth Schweikert's *Augen zu* are my own translations; the original German is given in footnotes in each case.
[4] Strigl calls Jenny "das wohl meistporträtierte Wunderfräulein des Blätterwalds" (Strigl 2001, 133).
[5] "Ich erhebe nicht den Anspruch, für eine ganze Generation zu sprechen, [...] aber ich scheine bei einigen den Nerv getroffen zu haben" (Jenny, quoted in Henning 1997).

tram. In candid prose, the child Jo tells us how he brings home women who listen to Mick Jagger on the record player, get drunk and fall asleep on her bedroom floor; and she explains how he helps her to go to sleep at night by tracing shapes in the dark with his glowing cigarettes. For all his failings, Jo's father is the more stable influence in her life; Jo's relationship with her mother, Lucy, is a lot less reliable. Lucy takes her daughter to stay with her every Sunday, but then leaves her with a babysitter while she goes out; once in a while, she picks her up from school to act as a decoy on a shoplifting trip to town. The only time that Jo is taken on an outing is when her mother takes her out into the forest to tell her that she has fallen in love with an artist and is leaving for good. The child Jo learns very early that the adults in her life cannot be relied upon, and she reacts by withdrawing into her own world.

The second part of Jenny's novel, and the main part of the narrative, deals with nineteen-year-old Jo, who has followed her mother abroad—we are never told where, although the placenames and climate would suggest that it is Italy—in an attempt to rekindle a relationship with her. However, Jo's mother, Lucy, is just as distant as before, and she refuses to talk about the past or to acknowledge her abandonment of her daughter. While Jo is visiting, Lucy's new husband, Alois, is killed in a car crash, a probable suicide. Lucy has a nervous breakdown and locks herself up in Alois's studio, where she has spread the pollen of countless fresh flowers—this is the pollen room of the title. After days calling out to her mother, Jo eventually breaks the windows of the studio with a shovel to reach her, but Lucy stands up and walks away from the room and refuses to talk about even this incident with her grown-up daughter.

Jo ends up staying two years with her mother, but when she finally accepts that Lucy is not willing or able to offer her the kind of relationship that she wants, she leaves and returns to Switzerland, disappointed and disillusioned. Arriving home again, she finds that her father has moved to the suburbs with his girlfriend, who is seven months pregnant with a baby girl. Anna, her father's girlfriend, picks Jo up from her train in "a real family car, the kind you can go on holiday in" (Jenny 1998, 148). And even the glowing cigarettes of her childhood years are gone, as Jo's father has given up smoking. Jo reacts to this final betrayal with anger. She turns her back on her father's new family and leaves, and the novel closes with Jo sitting alone on a park bench as the first snowflakes fall.

It is not surprising that *The Pollen Room* has often been read as a critique of the 1968 generation and all that it stands for (e.g. Reinacher

2003; Henning 1997; Köhler 1997). The young author reveals the deficits of her parents' generation—their grandiose ideas and their self-obsession that ignores those around them. At the same time, she highlights how in the 1990s, these self-styled radicals have sold their precious ideals for a station-wagon and a house in the suburbs. Yet Zoë Jenny does not criticise overtly, which is perhaps why she rejects this interpretation of her novel. The text points the finger at the 1968 generation, but it does so merely by describing in brutal clarity the point of view of the child who grows up in these circumstances. Father and mother are seen here from a different perspective—from the perspective of their children who have no respect for their empty gestures of revolt and their vanity (Reinacher 1997, 173).

*The Pollen Room* has been described as "an unsentimental, laconic view of what remains of the institution of the family at the end of this century" (Köhler 1997), and this is not without justification. Zoë Jenny insists that all of her novels are essentially about families and about conflict in families. "It's a fact," she says, "that my generation has the highest ever proportion of children whose parents are divorced. That leaves its mark" (Jenny, quoted in von Selchow 2002, 81). The image of the family that emerges in *The Pollen Room* is a fractured one; Jo's family is split by divorce and emigration and its members are marked by their traumatic experiences. This is particularly evident in the tenuous relationship between Jo and her mother Lucy.

Jo does not go into detail about the effect of her childhood abandonment on her life and relationships. However, there is some evidence in the writing that the trauma of neglect in early life has left its mark on the narrator. When depicting the moment when her mother tells her she is leaving, the child Jo describes how she reacts to this traumatic event by tuning her mother out and focusing instead on the humming and buzzing of the insects and the many sounds of the forest, perhaps in a gesture of self-protection. This reaction is replicated later in the novel; for example, when the teenager Jo is raped after a party, she reacts by focussing on a damp patch on the ceiling and the noises from the apartment above. This downplaying of significant and traumatic events in favour of the trivial is reflected in the writing as well; the separation of her parents, which was no doubt the defining moment of Jo's childhood, is reduced to a sub-clause in the opening paragraph of the narrative, which focuses instead on the details of the new living arrangements (Stocker 2002, 382). The lack of emotional closeness in Jo's early life is reflected in an extremely detached narrative style. The effects of her early trauma are thus woven into the fabric of the writing.

It is clear that the mother/daughter conflict is central to this narrative. In some measure, *The Pollen Room* can be read as a novel about the search both for a mother and for a lost ideal of motherhood. From early childhood, Jo's mother is an elusive figure in her life, more absent than she is present. Jo hangs onto those memories of childhood where she felt closest to her mother; for example, her mother's rituals as she gets ready to go out for the evening stand out in Jo's mind:

> In the evening she stood in front of the big mirror with her hair up, doing things to her face with little pencils and sponges. I passed her the little tubes and bottles that were on the windowsill, and unscrewed the expensive-looking flower- and drop-shaped stoppers of her scent bottles. The minute the babysitter arrived, she let down her hair so that it fanned out across her back in a sweet-smelling chestnut mass, and vanished into the night. (Jenny 1998, 14)

This moment of feminine interaction creates in the child Jo's mind an image of her mother as a beautiful, mysterious and intangible creature, and when, at the age of nineteen, she leaves her home to go in search of Lucy, it is this fantasy that drives her. On her arrival at Lucy's house, Jo describes her burning need to be a part of Lucy's life: "With the smooth white door in front of me, I thought how from now on Lucy's life would take place before my eyes, and no longer be that great secret, like a hungry beast of prey pitilessly chewing up the ground on which I meant to walk. The time had come for me at last to be an indispensable part of Lucy's life" (Jenny 1998, 70). Jo dreams of shared confidences, of whispered secrets and of the rekindling of a relationship that she and her mother never had.

In a sense, then, the demonisation of the mother figure in this novel is already predetermined by Jo's idealisation of mothering. How can Lucy ever be an acceptable mother to Jo when she can never live up to her daughter's ideal images of motherhood? Jo longs for a very traditional type of nurturing, the very opposite of all that her biological mother believes in and represents. She yearns to be part of a conventional, nuclear family: "I fall into a daydream in which I imagine I'm suddenly much younger, and Mum is in the kitchen making supper for us while I'm finishing my homework" (Jenny 1998, 59). She rejects Lucy, the modern, emancipated woman, in favour of a return to a very traditional form of mothering.[6]

From the outset, Lucy is marked as the archetypal "bad mother" due to her abandonment of her child in favour of her lover. She is a mother who rejects the role assigned to her by history, biology and society, and she rejects her child in the process. In this reversal of the Demeter/Persephone story, it is the daughter who leaves to go and search for her mother and to regain what was stolen. Lucy is presented as the antithesis of the traditional mother. She is youthful, vibrant and beautiful, sexually potent and a threat to Jo, rather than a loyal champion or a role model. This competition between the two is dramatised at one point. In a moment of generosity, Lucy takes Jo to her favourite place, and Jo takes this as a sign that her mother wants to make a place for her in her life. However, instead of bringing them closer together, the outing serves only to emphasise the estrangement between them: "Spray glittered in the air, thousands of rainbow-coloured droplets breaking in the light, and I was about to call Lucy to come in the water too when I saw her expression. She was scrutinising me like an enemy" (Jenny 1998, 46).

Lucy insists that Jo must call her by her first name and tell everyone that she is her sister and not her mother, denying both her biological relationship to Jo and the generation gap between them. In addition, she rejects their shared history: "She said she was not prepared to discuss the past with me. She felt she had no need to justify this position, and if I had anything I wanted to ask her about, she regretted she wouldn't be able to help me" (Jenny 1998, 52). Whilst Jo gives in to Lucy's demands, she is confused by what she experiences as a further abandonment: "A suspicion rises in me, and I'm suddenly dying to ask her if she's quite sure that it was she who left my father then and got on a plane. Or is there not some completely different version; and is she really sure that I came out of her belly. Because at this moment that seems completely impossible" (Jenny 1998, 58–9).

Many theorists have emphasised the importance of the mother figure—and notably the rejection of the mother—for the constitution of the daughter's identity (Nice 1992, 9). Irigaray put the case as follows: "The bond between mother and daughter, daughter and mother, must be

---

[6] It is interesting that when Jo is presented with the possibility of a traditional family with her father, she rejects it. Clearly, Jo's images of the ideal family are focussed on her mother and not her father.

broken so that the daughter can become woman" (Irigaray 1984, 161, quoted and translated in Hirsch 1989, 43). The question then arises: How can the daughter become woman if the bond between mother and daughter never existed to begin with? Seen thus, Jo's longing for a mother can be related to her search for her own identity. And Lucy is seen here as an obstacle in Jo's path, the mother who refuses to be a mother and thus refuses to allow her daughter to take the first steps towards womanhood.

The mother figure is certainly portrayed in a very negative light in this novel. However, we must take into account that everything in the narrative, all the events and happenings, are mediated through Jo, and thus, it is a very one-sided perspective that we are presented with. This novel calls attention to the power of the mother/daughter relationship, yet it does so almost entirely from the point of view of the traumatised daughter. In that sense, this novel does not correspond to the kind of feminist family romance that Marianne Hirsch envisions and that will allow for a new and different articulation of the maternal perspective. Rather, it focuses entirely on the point of view of the daughter and denies that of the mother.

There are some indications in this text that Lucy too has suffered, though these are played down in the narrative. For example, the child Jo describes her mother's return from a night out:

I was woken up later by her whimpering, and felt my way across to her bed in the dark. She lay under the colourful flower-patterned bedspread, shaken by secret griefs I couldn't understand. All I could see of her face was the little triangle from her mouth to the tip of her nose, all the rest was covered by her white hands. After a while, she drew back the cover, and I crept into her salty warm bed with her. (Jenny 1998, 14–15)

However, whether it is due to Lucy's unwillingness to go back over old territory, or whether it is due to her own hurt and anger at her mother's abandonment of her, the grown-up Jo seems unwilling or unable to see beyond her own pain and understand her mother's side of the story.

This novel does not by any means present the kind of "double voice" that Hirsch calls for, a "voice that would yield a multiple female consciousness" (Hirsch 1989, 161). On the contrary, I would suggest that the power play that is present in the content of the text is re-enacted and inverted in its form. The mother's story is subsumed into that of the daughter, and this is a narrative act that allows the daughter to take control of her mother's voice. Thus, although on the level of the content, Jo never succeeds in gaining the upper hand in her relationship with her mother, on a formal level, she assumes the position of authority and takes control of her narrative.

## RUTH SCHWEIKERT, AUGEN ZU

Zoë Jenny's *The Pollen Room* points, albeit vaguely, to the issue of maternal suffering and the difficulties of retaining one's subjectivity as mother; however, the fact that Lucy is denied a voice in the narrative means that Jenny's novel does not really offer any new insights into the maternal perspective. Ruth Schweikert's *Augen zu*, published in 1998, is a far more complex text, both in terms of its polyphonic narrative technique and in the way it envisions motherhood and the potential for maternal subjectivity. The title, *Augen zu* [Close your eyes], alludes to the German expression "Augen zu und durch." This expression would most often be offered as counsel to someone who has to face difficult circumstances, advising them to accept the inevitability of the situation and focus on getting through it. Schweikert's novel foregrounds the roles women play and the challenges they face within families, within society and in narrative; its title implies that the only way a woman can cope with these difficulties is simply to close her eyes and get on with it.

It is noteworthy that Ruth Schweikert has not been identified as closely with the literary "Fräuleinwunder" (Hage 1999) as Zoë Jenny. Schweikert was twenty-nine when she published her first collection of short stories, *Erdnüsse. Totschlagen* (1994), the same collection that captivated Beatrice von Matt. These short stories deal with dysfunctional families, the silent suffering of women and the complexity of mother-daughter relationships, and thus they already introduce the issues that are the focus of her novel *Augen zu*, published four years later. If Schweikert's short story collection drew attention to her talent, her debut novel established her as a leading light on the Swiss literary scene.

*Augen zu* centres on one day in the life of the protagonist, Aleks Martin Schwarz, who lives in Zurich and is the single mother of two sons, Oliver and Lukas. Aleks's life revolves around her fragile little family, her rather unsuccessful career as an artist and her handsome, French-born lover Raoul Lieben. This particular day, 16th June 1995, is a significant day for Aleks; apart from being her 30th birthday, it is also the day she conceives a child with Raoul—a child that she will lose before its birth—and the day her mother, Doris, takes the drug overdose that will result in her death two days later. This one day in Aleks's life thus encapsulates the themes and ideas on which the narrative also hinges—the process of coming to motherhood; the loss of identity that seems to go hand in hand with the role of mother; and concerns with growing older, in particular growing older as a woman.

Through a series of flashbacks and flash-forwards and through an unusual, polyphonic narrative perspective, the novel also gives us an insight into the past, present and future of Aleks's family and those connected to her. Thus, we learn that Aleks was born Alexandra Heinrich, in a small town not far from Zurich, referred to in the novel only as "the small town."[7] Her father, Alexander Jakob Heinrich, known to all, even to his wife, as Heinrich, is a diffident academic with high expectations for his children and a Latin proverb for every situation. Her younger brothers, Tom and Andreas, born only eleven months apart, are close enough to be twins, and they let no one into their private world. Aleks's mother, Doris, a German who came to Switzerland after the war, has devoted her life to her husband and her children. As a reward for her years of dedication, Doris is eventually abandoned by her family; Aleks leaves home at eighteen, and both of Doris's sons move in with their girlfriends around the same time that her husband, after thirty years of marriage, leaves her for another woman.

Aleks's upbringing bears all the signs of middle-class conventionality, but Aleks is marked from the outset as unusual. "You're just different, said her father; you have the intellect of a man in a body that's slowly developing into a woman's."[8] In her early teens, Alexandra changes her name to the more masculine-sounding Aleks in silent protest against her emerging femininity. Alexandra/Aleks wages war on her changing body, refusing even to eat for fear of growing into a woman. She hopes to hold off puberty and her physical maturity by sheer force of will: "I don't want to become a woman, Aleks said to herself, so I won't become a woman. I don't want to get my period so I won't get it."[9] Yet Aleks soon finds that will power is not enough and that her development into womanhood is inevitable.

[7] The German version of the novel refers to the town as "die Kleine Stadt" (Schweikert 1998, 61).

[8] "Du bist eben anders, sagte der Vater, du hast den Verstand eines Mannes im langsam sich ausbildenden Körper einer Frau" (Schweikert 1998, 74–75).

[9] "Ich will keine Frau werden, sagte sich Aleks, also werde ich auch keine Frau. Ich will keine Periode kriegen, also kriege ich auch keine" (Schweikert 1998, 125).

Despite the fact that Aleks does not want to grow up to be a woman, she is somehow fascinated by her emerging sexuality and consciously puts herself in dangerous situations to test it out. For example, she often walks alone in the evening along the riverbank, in an area where a rapist is known to prowl for victims (Schweikert 1998, 131). On one occasion during her teenage years, she very deliberately flirts with three middle-aged men; she agrees to a drink with them and even gets into their car. Here, she has her first experience of French kissing, but she loses her nerve when it looks like things might progress further: "So as not to be raped, she threw the car door open at the last minute and ran to the Catholic youth club, where she had spent the evening in lively debate and been picked up a few minutes later, as arranged, by her mother, who just looked at her. Her face glowed with shame, hurt and unacknowledged desire."[10]

Aleks's mother can only look on helplessly as her daughter fights so hard against her sexual identity and the social roles that are bound to it. She is dismayed when one of Aleks's teachers recommends that Aleks sees a psychiatrist and even pays for Aleks's twice-weekly visits to a psychologist in Zurich from her housekeeping money to hide this fact from Aleks's father. In particular, Doris is horrified at Aleks's compulsive self-harming, and she is filled with shame and dread at the scars on Aleks's lower arms from the kitchen knife: "At least put on a long-sleeved pullover, said Doris Heinrich with a helpless tenderness, please! That's all I'm asking, do you hear?"[11]

It is clear that many of Aleks's fears about becoming a woman revolve around her mother and what she perceives as her weakness and subjection. In Hirsch's terms, Aleks expresses the "daughter's anger at the mother who has accepted her powerlessness, who is unable to protect her from a submission to society's gender arrangements" (Hirsch 1989, 165). Aleks has little respect for her mother, whom she depicts almost exclusively in negative terms: she describes her reluctance to look "into the powerless eyes of her own mother [...] who was still standing there with her arms

---

[10] "Um nicht vergewaltigt zu werden, riß sie in letzter Minute die Autotür auf und rannte zum katholischen Jugendhaus, wo sie den Abend mit lebhaften Diskussionen verbracht hatte und Minuten später verabredungsgemäß von der Mutter abgeholt wurde, die sie nur ansah. Ihr Gesicht glühte vor Scham, Verletzung und uneingestandener Lust" (Schweikert 1998, 134).

[11] "Zieh dir wenigstens einen langärmeligen Pullover darüber, sagte Doris Heinrich so hilflos sanft; bitte! Ich bitte dich nur darum, hörst du?" (Schweikert 1998, 127).

hanging down and calling her name."[12] On more than one occasion in the novel, Aleks refers to her mother as being childlike; her eyes are described as "mother's grown-up children's eyes" and her hands as "her small children's hands."[13] Doris does all she can to reach out to her daughter and to smooth her passage into womanhood, but Aleks is unable or unwilling to let her mother inside her private world.

What is particularly fascinating about Schweikert's interrogation of the mother-daughter complex in this novel is that it not only offers us the daughter's perspective on her mother; its shifting narrative perspective also affords us insight into the mother's perspective on her life and on her changing relationship with her grown-up daughter. Thus, we learn that Doris Heinrich has suffered much in her early years and that her childhood trauma has had a profound effect on her later life. Born in the German city of Freiburg in 1931, Doris lost her mother and her brother after the city was bombed in the early hours of the 27th November 1944. A month later, Doris's father decided to overcome his grief by attempting to kill himself and his daughter, without success. After this incident, Doris goes to live with an aunt, and she manages to get work in a hotel in Basle when the war comes to an end. It is here that she meets Aleks's father, Heinrich, and when he asks her to marry him, she doesn't hesitate. However, despite her new start in a new country with her new husband, Doris is still haunted by the ghosts of her past, and her way of coping with her sorrow is to drown it in alcohol. From the early days of her marriage, Doris is a regular drinker, though she does her best to hide this from her husband and her children. When she is finally left alone in the house in her later years, she can devote herself wholeheartedly to the alcoholism that she was barely able to conceal when her children were younger. At the age of sixty-four, she now spends her days cleaning her big, empty house and her evenings drinking herself into oblivion.

Ironically, Doris's drinking serves as a platform for a brief but important connection between mother and daughter. When Aleks, at the age of twelve, finds her mother passed out on the bedroom floor after a bout of drinking, her reaction is to take control of the situation; in a curious

---

[12] Aleks describes the difficulty "in die kraftlosen Augen der eigenen Mutter zu schauen, die noch immer mit herabhängenden Armen dastand und ihren Namen rief" (Schweikert 1998, 98–99).

[13] Doris's eyes are described as "Mutters erwachsene Kinderaugen" (Schweikert 1998, 49) and her hands as "ihre rechten Kinderhände" (Schweikert 1998, 110).

role-reversal, she takes on the position of mother to her younger brothers, preparing them something to eat and discouraging them from disturbing their mother. As Pia Reinacher remarks, "The perspective has changed. The child seeking protection now steps in to support the maternal figure who has fallen apart."[14] It is paradoxical that Aleks seems to find it easier to accept and acknowledge her mother when she drinks; at one point, we are told, "When her mother had been drinking, Aleks even sometimes found it easy to love her."[15] Doris's alcoholism enables her daughter to see her as a human being, rather than merely as a mother whose sole function is to serve her husband and care for her children.

In this way, *Augen zu* focuses on what it means to be a mother and on how becoming a mother relates to a loss of individual identity. Hirsch comments on this process as follows: "The adult woman who is a mother, in particular, continues to exist only in relation to her child, never as a subject in her own right" (Hirsch 1989, 167). Schweikert's novel interrogates the gradual erasure of subjectivity that seems to be inextricably bound to the role of mother through the figures of Doris and Aleks. As far as her children are concerned, Doris Heinrich no longer exists as an individual, but only as "Mameeee," complete with "the hysterical spiky ee-sound of her own childish cries, repeated nigh-on ten thousand times."[16] As a mother, Doris has become estranged even from her own sexuality: "She wore white strappy sandals with narrow high heels and figure-hugging stretch jeans with low-cut, tight-fitting t-shirts; she sat down, crossed one leg over the other, jiggled her feet, and projected outward all of the pent-up sexuality that she probably kept concealed from herself." [17] In the same way, Aleks finds that when she becomes a mother, her identity is also subsumed by that of her sons, and she too experiences a loss of individuality. At one point in the narrative, while she watches her children eat the meal she has prepared for them, she is reminded of her own

---

[14] "Die Perspektive hat sich verdreht. Das schutzsuchende Kind richtet sich auf über der mütterlichen Instanz, die zusammengebrochen ist" (Reinacher 1998, 2).

[15] "Wenn die Mutter getrunken hatte, war es Aleks früher manchmal beinahe leicht gefallen, sie zu lieben" (Schweikert 1998, 95).

[16] "das hysterisch spitze ii ihres eigenen, wohl zehntausendfach wiederholten Kinderschreis" (Schweikert 1998, 127).

[17] "[Sie] trug […] weiße Riemchensandalen mit dünnen, hohen Absätzen und figurbetonte Stretchjeans, dazu weit ausgeschnittene, enganliegende T-Shirts; sie setzte sich hin, schlug die Bein übereinander, wippte mit den Füßen und stülpte ihre ganze unerlöste Sexualität nach außen, die sie vor sich selber wohl versteckt hielt" (Schweikert 1998, 25).

mother's attempts to convince her brothers to eat dinner, and for a moment, their lives are united. Moreover, Aleks, similar to her mother, resorts to taking prescription drugs "just to be able to keep going and maintain some sense of balance."[18]

However, it should be noted that Schweikert's novel does not stop at describing the way in which a woman can lose her identity through motherhood; it also explores the potential for regaining that identity and for reanimating the position of the mother in discourse. In *Augen zu*, Doris Heinrich ultimately reacts against her abandonment by the husband and children she has sacrificed herself for. While visiting Doris in the house that was once their family home, Heinrich brings his former wife a present of a stained-glass picture of a saint. Doris's reaction to this gift is quite different from what Heinrich was expecting:

> Doris held the stained-glass picture with Saint Martin up to the light, looked at the round bald patch on her husband's scalp and felt an urge to whack the shining, colourful glass picture on his head, just so she wouldn't have to look at his ludicrous vulnerability anymore. Instead, her skinny arms started hitting out. They hit and hit and kept hitting until the glass picture shattered on the floor; her little fists kept on hitting as Heinrich sat paralysed, cowering on the kitchen chair that was described in the furniture-store brochure as contemporary rustic, his hands over his eyes.[19]

Doris's act of violence in breaking the stained-glass picture can be seen as an expression of her anger against her husband and children, who have taken the best years of her life and abandoned her when she needs them most. This gesture can simultaneously be read as an aggressive act of reclaiming a subjectivity that she has been denied in her role as wife and mother. In effect, through this act of rebellion, she re-establishes herself as an individual. Hirsch describes both the inevitability of maternal anger and its problematic consequences: "The projected angry mother of the

---

[18] "bloß um grundlos ausgeglichen weiterleben zu können" (Schweikert 1998, 29).

[19] "Doris hielt die Wappenscheibe mit dem heiligen Martin ans Licht, blickte auf den in der Mitte kahlen Schädel ihres Ehemannes und wollte ihm bloß, um dessen lächerlich anmutende Verletzbarkeit nicht mehr sehen zu müssen, die leuchtend bunte Wappenscheibe auf den Kopf legen. Statt dessen schlugen ihre dünnen Arme zu. Sie schlugen einfach. Schlugen, bis die Wappenscheibe am Boden zersprang; ihre kleinen Fäuste schlugen weiter, während Heinrich wie gelähmt auf den neuen hölzernen, im Möbel Pfister-Prospekt als modern-rustikal bezeichneten Küchenstuhl hocken blieb, die Hände vor den Augen" (Schweikert 1998, 48).

psychoanalytic narrative, then, would react to the child's so-called inevitable hostility with anger of her own, would feel wronged when, after years of nurturing and care, she is left behind. Should she rebel, however, should she express her own feelings about an enforced and inevitable separation, she would cease to be maternal" (Hirsch 1989, 170).[20] Indeed, Heinrich interprets Doris's act as an expression of madness, and as a result of her outburst, he has her admitted to a psychiatric clinic the same day.

It is significant that Doris's violent outburst facilitates a rapprochement of sorts between mother and daughter, and Aleks can at last learn to see things from her mother's perspective. On the day Doris is taken away to the clinic, Aleks returns home to her mother's house with her two sons. In her mother's kitchen, she prepares a meal for her sons and contemplates the events from her mother's past that have led to this day: "Aleks looked out the kitchen window into the garden and at the withered apricot trees that had long ago grown taller than her, fried the potatoes into rösti, seasoned the meat, ate and suddenly wished she could change places with her mother, wished she could wake up with mother's childish eyes and see her devastated world on the evening of the 27th November 1944."[21] It seems that it is only when Doris rebels against the dictates of her role as mother that Aleks can finally begin to appreciate her as an individual, with a past and an identity of her own.

In a sense, Doris's suicide can also be interpreted as an active, even aggressive attempt to regain her identity. Evidently, it is an act of violence against herself, not dissimilar from Aleks's self-harming, but there are no indications in the text to suggest that her suicide is born of self-loathing or self-pity; paradoxically, Doris's overdose can be interpreted as a final attempt to regain her own subjectivity, to "speak," as it were, as a subject. This idea is compounded by the fact that Doris leaves behind a letter to be read by her family after her death, a letter which finally tells the story of

---

[20] Hirsch also recognises the problematic nature of discussing maternal anger: "I recognize that, in privileging anger, I represent maternal subjectivity from one, limited vantage point, and one that converges with cultural representations of the maternal. Yet I suspect that such a vantage point is unavoidable since anger may well be what defines subjectivity whenever the subject is denied speech" (Hirsch 1989, 170).

[21] "Aleks sah aus dem Küchenfenster in den Garten, dessen verblühte Aprikosenbäume ihr längst über den Kopf gewachsen waren, briet die Kartoffeln zu Rösti, würzte das Fleisch, aß und wünschte sich plötzlich, mit ihrer Mutter den Blick zu tauschen, mit Mutters erwachsenen Kinderaugen zu erwachen und ihre zerstörte Welt zu sehen am Abend des siebenundzwanzigsten November 1944" (Schweikert 1998, 49).

her loss of her family. Whilst Aleks's brothers are irritated that Doris has chosen this moment to reveal the secrets of her past—"her whole life long she just made vague references and then she leaves us to deal with her shitty misery alone"[22]—Aleks feels only compassion for what her mother has suffered.

Schweikert's novel thus differs significantly from Zoë Jenny's exploration of the mother-daughter relationship, in that it leaves room for the articulation of a "double voice," in line with Marianne Hirsch's definition of what that means (Hirsch 1989, 161). We hear from both daughter and mother in this complex family romance. Although Aleks is undoubtedly the central figure in this novel, narrative authority is not given to one character over the other; neither character is prioritised and neither position is favoured. Aleks and Doris are represented as both mothers and daughters, subjects as daughters and denied subjectivity as mothers. Doris's rebellion against the dictates of her role as mother allows Aleks to approach her as a speaking subject, and mother and daughter can finally speak to each other as subjects in their own right.

It is interesting to note that in one flash-forward, we learn that after the loss of her first child with Raoul, Aleks will go on to conceive and give birth to a healthy baby girl. Only brief mention is made of Aleks's daughter, Jael, born two years after Doris's death and after the central events in the narrative. However, this allusion to Aleks's own daughter is significant, since it suggests a cyclical quality and an open-endedness to the novel. The narrative of mothers and daughters will not end, it suggests, with Doris's death and the end of the relationship between Doris and Aleks; rather, it will continue on into the next generation.

Ruth Schweikert's *Augen zu* demonstrates that the new wave of literature by women that emerged in German-language literature in the 1990s, the so-called "Fräuleinwunder" (Hage 1999), offers some new perspectives on the themes and motifs that had preoccupied women writers for generations. Schweikert's novel concentrates its attention on the subjectivity of women, but it does so without excluding the maternal perspective; rather, it interrogates in a very deliberate way the loss of agency associated with the role of mother and envisions strategies for the reclamation of the mother's subjectivity. It allows for a space where mothers and daughters can speak to each other, and thus answers Marianne Hirsch's

---

[22] "Ihr Leben lang hat sie bloß geheimnisvolle Andeutungen gemacht, um uns dann mit ihrem beschissenen Elend allein zu lassen" (Schweikert 1998, 118).

call for "a feminist family romance of mothers *and* daughters, both subjects, speaking to each other and living in familial and communal contexts
which enable the subjectivity of each member" (Hirsch 1989, 163).

## CONCLUSION

The new generation of young women writers that emerged in the German-
speaking world in the late 1990s was celebrated by critics as signalling a
break with the past and a new approach to topics that preoccupied women
writers of the previous generation. While German critic Volker Hage
praised these young women for initiating a "new culture of storytelling,"[23]
Swiss critic Beatrice von Matt credited the emerging writers in German-
speaking Switzerland with introducing "new ways of writing" (Von Matt
1998a: 59). This chapter has looked in particular at debut novels by two
of the writers who are considered to be representative of this new generation of authors, Zoë Jenny and Ruth Schweikert, and it has sought to
probe the extent and the ways in which their work offers a new perspective
on a topic that has traditionally preoccupied women writers. Both novels
foreground the relationship between mother and daughter, which has
long been central to women's fiction but which has, according to Marianne
Hirsch, always tended to privilege the daughter's perspective over that of
the mother. As this analysis has shown, Jenny's novel *The Pollen Room*
ultimately falls into this trap; although the text alludes to the personal suffering of the maternal figure, her trauma is subsumed by her daughter's
narrative of maternal abandonment. Seen from Hirsch's perspective, this
is deeply problematic, since it continues a tradition of consigning mothers
to the position of objects within their daughter's narratives. In Schweikert's
*Augen zu*, on the other hand, the shifting narrative perspective means that
we gain equal insight into the mother's and daughter's view points, allowing us to understand the parallels between their experiences and the rich
connections between their interrelated subjectivities. In this way,
Schweikert's novel belongs with those contemporary novels identified by
Hirsch as offering a way forward for women's writing at the cusp of the
twenty-first century.

---

[23] Hage writes about the advent of "eine neue Erzählkultur" in Germany (Hage 1999: 245).

## REFERENCES

Caemmerer, Christine, Walter Delabar, and Helga Meise. 2005. *Fräuleinwunder literarisch. Literatur von Frauen zu Beginn des 21. Jahrhunderts.*, Inter-Lit. Vol. 6. Frankfurt: Peter Lang.

Hage, Volker. 1999. Ganz schön abgedreht. *Der Spiegel* No. 12, 22.03.1999.

Henning, Peter. 1997. Familiäre Abgründe. *Focus* 8 September.

Hirsch, Marianne. 1989. *The Mother/Daughter Plot. Narrative, Psychoanalysis, Feminism.* Bloomington: Indiana U.P.

Irigaray, Luce. 1984. *Éthique de la différence sexuelle.* Paris: Minuit.

Jenny, Zoë. 1998. *The Pollen Room.* Translated by Michael Hoffmann. London: Bloomsbury. [Originally published as *Das Blütenstaubzimmer*- Frankfurt: Frankfurter Verlagsanstalt, 1997.]

Klages, Norgard. 1995. *Look back in anger: Mother-daughter and Father-daughter relationships in women's autobiographical writings of the 1970s and 1980s.* New York: Peter Lang.

Kocher, Ursula. 2005. Die Leere und die Angst – Erzählen "Fräuleinwunder" anders? Narrative Techniken bei Judith Hermann, Zoë Jenny und Jenny Erpenbeck. In *Fräuleinwunder literarisch*, ed. Caemmerer et al., 53–72. Frankfurt: Peter Lang.

Köhler, Andrea. 1997. Abschied von den Eltern. Zoë Jennys Roman-Début *Das Blütenstaubzimmer*. *NZZ* 6/7 September: 47.

Müller, Heidelinde. 2004. *Das "literarische Fräuleinwunder". Inspektion eines Phänomens der deutschen Gegenwartsliteratur in Einzelfallstudien.*, Inter-Lit Vol. 5. Frankfurt: Peter Lang.

Nice, Vivien E. 1992. *Mothers and Daughters. The Distortion of a Relationship.* London: Macmillan.

Reinacher, Pia. 1997. Die Lebenslügen der Eltern. *Tages-Anzeiger* 5 September: 89.

———. 1998. Die Frau als ein sinnlicher Augentrost. *Tages-Anzeiger (Buchzeichen)* 07 (10): 1–2.

———. 2003. *Je Suisse. Zur aktuellen Lage der Schweizer Literatur.* Munich/Vienna: Nagel & Kimche.

Schweikert, Ruth. 1994. *Erdnüsse. Totschlagen. Erzählungen.* Zurich: Rotpunktverlag.

———. 1998. *Augen zu.* Ammann: Zürich.

Stocker, Günther. 2002. Traumen des Aufwachsens. Drei Variationen aus der Schweizer Literatur der neunziger Jahre. *Weimarer Beiträge* 48 (2): 380–398.

Strigl, Daniela. 2001. Fräulein- und andere Wunder. Galvagni, Röggla & Co. In *Geschlechter. Essays zur Gegenwartsliteratur*, ed. Freidbert Aspetsberger and Konstanze Fliedl, 131–151. Innsbruck: Studien.

Von Matt, Beatrice. 1998a. "New Women's Writing in German-speaking Switzerland" 25 *Years of Emancipation?* In *Women in Switzerland 1971–1996,* ed. Joy Charnley, Malcolm Pender, and Andrew Wilkin, 57–71. Bern: Peter Lang.

———. 1998b. *Frauen schreiben die Schweiz. Aus der Literaturgeschichte der Gegenwart.* Frauenfeld/Stuttgart/Wien: Huber.

Von Selchow, Stephanie. 2002. Beim Schreiben muss man sich die Maske vom Gesicht reissen. Zoë Jenny über ihr Leben als junge Schriftstellerin, den ehrlichen Blick und die Wertschätzung des kulturellen Lebens. *Siehst du den Horizont? Franka Potente, Zoë Jenny, Franzi von Almsick, Melanie Rohde, Renate Schmidt u.v.a. über ihr Leben.* 74–84. Aarau: Sauerländer.

# CHAPTER 8

# Contested Motherhood in Autobiographical Writing: Rachel Cusk and Sheila Heti

*Margaretha Fahlgren and Anna Williams*

Whenever I pick up a new book by a woman I check the author biography on the back flap to see whether she has children. I'm not entirely sure why I do this and what, exactly, I am trying to gauge, but I think it has something to do with an abiding interest in how other women writers have arranged their lives and enabled their ambitions: Do they view writing as a sacrosanct vocation and themselves as secular nuns of a sort, for whom few distractions—especially one as time-filling as motherhood—are to be allowed? Or do they accept their creative aspirations as part of a larger, often messy whole that includes a child or children?

This publication has received funding from the European Union's Horizon 2020 research and innovation programme under grant agreement No 952366, and from the Centre for Gender Research and the Department of Literature at Uppsala University.

M. Fahlgren • A. Williams (✉)
Department of Literature, Uppsala University, Uppsala, Sweden
e-mail: margaretha.fahlgren@littvet.uu.se; anna.williams@littvet.uu.se

© The Author(s) 2023
H. Wahlström Henriksson et al. (Eds.), *Narratives of Motherhood and Mothering in Fiction and Life Writing*, Palgrave Macmillan Studies in Family and Intimate Life,
https://doi.org/10.1007/978-3-031-17211-3_8

135

These questions are posed by the American writer and critic Daphne Merkin (2021, 27), and her curious inquiry highlights a crucial subject in contemporary literature. A wide range of fiction, autobiographical writing, and feminist theory on motherhood have shaped a new textual landscape (Podnieks and O'Reilly 2010). Some contributions to this landscape have even caused heated media debates.

Motherhood is a universal phenomenon as well as an urgent field of scholarly and scientific inquiry. It is a recurring theme in literature and life writing, which frequently scrutinize controversial issues with unsparing candor. Literature about the troublesome aspects of motherhood or about whether or not to become a mother have provoked especially intense discussions. Such discussions may well be responses to the critical assumption made by the French historian Élisabeth Badinter (2011), that the role of the mother has emerged as the most important in women's lives in recent decades, thus undermining feminist progress. In this chapter we examine contemporary autobiographical narratives which explore the notion of motherhood as the central issue in women's lives. These narratives have been important in offering alternative discourses and thereby broadening the concept of motherhood. We discuss them in the light of motherhood studies (DiQuinzio 1999; Podnieks and O'Reilly 2010; Badinter 2011), and theories about matrilineal narratives in contemporary literature (Yu 2005).

Works by two highly acclaimed Canadian writers are at the center of our study: Rachel Cusk's *A Life's Work: On Becoming a Mother* (first published in 2001, 2008) and Sheila Heti's *Motherhood* (2018).[1] When Rachel Cusk published *A Life's Work* about her personal experiences of motherhood, the text stirred an emotional response among reviewers in which she was measured against an ideal image of the good mother and accused of narcissism. Similar to Cusk, Sheila Heti's *Motherhood* concentrates on the self in its poignant and philosophical inquiry into motherhood, relationships, and work, and into the impact of the choice to have or not have a child. Both volumes lean on emotions as well as intellectual argument, and ambivalence toward motherhood is striking in both works.

We follow two main lines of theoretical inquiry in our analysis of Cusk's and Heti's works. Firstly, we focus on what the literary scholar Toril Moi has identified in contemporary life writing as the "exercise of attention" (Moi 2017b). For the philosophical concept of attention she refers to Iris

[1] The study emanates from the research project "Mother Anyway: Literary, Medical and Media Narratives" (Dept. of Literature, Uppsala University), funded by the Swedish Research Council, 2017–2019.

Murdoch and Simone Weil, and observes that it is an important feature in prominent literature. It concerns a certain ability of attention, of responding to reality, on the part of the writer which in turn can inspire the reader to become more attentive to both reality and literature (Moi 2017a, 17–22, 14 f., 64).

One of Moi's literary examples is the acclaimed Norwegian author Karl Ove Knausgaard in his autobiographical account *My Struggle* (2009–2011). In her reading, Moi observes how Knausgaard centers his attention on his ongoing life and uses description as an "exercise of attention." Writing about his everyday life makes him aware of his own existence. What characterizes his style, according to Moi, is that he "insists on the importance of feelings without buying into the language of affects" (Moi 2017b).

We view both Cusk and Heti as similarly endeavoring to understand the existential condition of the self in relation to motherhood by exploring their everyday experiences. Their investigations acknowledge the deep impact of emotions while formulating questions with artistic accuracy: Is becoming a mother equivalent to losing one's sense of self and identity as a writer? What will remain of the life they know and appreciate? In the case of Sheila Heti, the "exercise of attention" is primarily focused on her intellectual and emotional exploration, pursued while life goes on day by day. Rachel Cusk puts her attention to the reading of child manuals and observing what others, mothers, and medical staff convey to her about motherhood.

Secondly, the texts by Cusk and Heti bring to the fore the feminist examination of the definition of motherhood and mothering in a social context. In her groundbreaking book *Of Woman Born: Motherhood as Experience and Institution* (1976), Adrienne Rich defined the concepts by both sharing her own personal experiences of mothering and displaying how they were regulated by the patriarchal institution of motherhood. Sociologist Tina Miller continues the investigation in *Making Sense of Motherhood: A Narrative Approach* (2005), where she brings forward what she calls "cultural scripts"—discourses that affect societal and subjective views on motherhood and gender. Miller's definition of the more existentially oriented "motherhood"—different from "mothering"—takes into account the broad context of a complex phenomenon:

'Motherhood' on the other hand refers to the context in which motherhood takes place and is experienced. The institution of motherhood in the Western world is, then, historically, socially, culturally, politically and, importantly, *morally*, shaped. In turn, it powerfully shapes our experiences as women, whether or not we become mothers, because of the cultural assumptions related to women's desire to be mothers. (Miller 2005, 3)

Knowledge about reproduction and motherhood is shaped by "cultural scripts"—discourses in different times and environments which are especially strong if sanctioned and supported by structural conditions in society. Miller puts it thus: "where dominant cultural scripts are underpinned by social structures and practices which serve to reinforce and legitimise them, they become accepted as the 'normal' or 'natural' way to do things and, as a result, may be difficult to resist" (2005, 29).

As feminist research has shown, women's identities are still closely linked to their reproductive ability, whether or not they become mothers (Miller 2005, 54 f.). A woman without child is the exception that needs to be explained or examined. This means that cultural scripts on motherhood are especially difficult to resist, since they are closely related to female identity.

Additionally, cultural scripts about motherhood are not easily modified. They are closely linked to the idea of the good mother (a figure properly challenged in *A Life's Work*). As Patrice DiQuinzio (1999) has observed, the perception of modern motherhood is divided, immersed as it is in policies for equal opportunities, on the one hand, and, on the other, the focus on woman's exclusive biological relationship with the child.

Our goal is to shed light on how the texts discussed here relate to—and to a certain extent rewrite—cultural scripts about motherhood. We examine how the autobiographical subjects describe their lives and what they pay attention to, from the assumptions that motherhood is still a contested field and that women's identity is still to a large extent attached to their reproductive capacity. We argue that the questions of motherhood and mothering in the texts are delineated as a dynamic negotiation between individual, social, and political circumstances. Thus, we pay attention to both style and ideological content in order to understand how the writers communicate and evaluate their personal experiences of the deeply existential issues of motherhood and mothering.

## THE SOCIAL AND BIOLOGICAL QUESTION: WOMEN AND MOTHERHOOD

Sheila Heti's *Motherhood* has been labeled a novel, but it is obviously a hybrid between novel, memoir, and autobiography. Lara Feigel (2018) identifies its most novel-like characteristics as the use of the present-tense narration and the assumption that "the book knows more than the narrator does." Heti herself calls her work a "wrestling place" (2018, 284). There are obvious similarities between writer and narrator, but we will refer to the narrator as "Sheila" and consider her as a protagonist which is not necessarily identical with the author.

The book is an intimate account of a difficult time where Sheila—thirty-six years old when the story begins—finds herself at a decisive moment in life: the biological clock is ticking and she has to figure out whether or not she wants to become a mother. Her literary quest for an answer is made not only through reading, thinking, and talking to friends and her boy-friend Miles but also through the unconventional method of flipping coins. She poses a question ("Am I handling my relationship wrong?"), flips a coin, and receives a simple yes or no. This unusual practice contributes to the structure of this first-person narrative and creates a suggestive trajectory of chance, determinism, and coincidence.

*Motherhood* touches upon most of the contextual aspects observed by Tina Miller and illustrates how the institution of motherhood "shapes our experiences as women" (Miller 2005, 3). At the core of Heti's inquiry is the question of whether motherhood is a biological instinct or a socially constructed demand imposed on women. The protagonist's first priority is writing, and she realizes that a child would have irrevocable consequences for her way of life. A thought-provoking reflection deals with the regulating aspects of gender identity. Dwelling on her writing, Sheila feels guilty about prioritizing art over motherhood: "Maybe I have to think about myself less as a woman with this woman's special task, and more as an individual with her own special task—not put *woman* before my individuality" (25). This brings to light an important difference between male and female artists that was thoroughly addressed by women writers in the nineteenth century, as they grew more visible in the literary field. Up until the present, female artists have systematically been identified by their gender to a much larger extent than male writers who constitute the norm. It has been necessary for women to take into account their gender identity, both due to their subordinate position and because of biology. Traditionally they were responsible for taking care of the family, and if they chose a life devoted to art, many declined marriage and children.

The conflict between being a creative person, a writer, and a mother is likewise explored in Rachel Cusk's *A Life's Work*. When the story begins she is already pregnant. Being a writer, "a modern privileged woman," she has not reflected on the implications of biology. Not until she becomes pregnant does she realize that she cannot escape biology and bodily changes. She feels as if she has boarded a train which is heading toward "a vista of unfamiliar hills, leaving everything vanishing behind it" (25). Her pregnancy starts the journey to motherhood, an unknown territory which Cusk explores as a writer.

When her book was republished in 2008 Cusk wrote an introduction in which she addressed the vehement criticism of the book when it was first issued in 2001. Cusk dismisses the criticism, insisting that the book was never intended to be a "childcare manual." Instead, it is "governed by the subject *I*, not *You*" (4). The focus is not on the reader or the child, the book deals with the self in the light of motherhood: "I wrote it because I am a writer, and the experience of ambivalence that characterises the early stages of parenthood seemed to me to be kith and kin of the writer's fundamental ambivalence towards life; an ambivalence that is obscured by the organised social systems human communities devise, and that the writer or artist is always trying to recover and resolve" (4).

Cusk acknowledges the conflict between her identity as a writer and as a mother only when she becomes a mother, whereas Sheila in *Motherhood* wants to resolve this conflict before she decides whether or not to be a mother. After a talk with Miles, in which he declares that it is impossible to combine art and parenthood and succeed with both, Sheila admits to feeling sad, despite agreeing with him. "All morning I felt a kind of coldness in my chest towards him. Why must I be one of the people he's talking about?" (36) The narrative underscores how the self and the social cannot be separated, and it is done by laying bare Sheila's emotional response which opens up for different reactions.

*Motherhood* dwells upon not only the social and biological pressure of motherhood but also the idea that not wanting to have children might be a biological or even a sexual orientation in its own right, comparable to the desire to have them—obviously a thought-provoking argument which challenges the script of woman as a natural mother figure. When conveying this reflection, Sheila immediately connects it to her personal experience, a recollection of how as a child she perceived the world and her existential position in it:

> Wanting not to have children could even be called a sexual orientation, for what is more tied to sex than the desire to procreate or not? I suspect the intensity of this desire lies deep within our cells, and then there is all that culture adds, and that other people add, which skews our innate desires. I can look back at being a tiny child and see that I did not want children then.

I remember sitting at the kitchen table with my entire family, and suddenly knowing that I would never be a mother, for I was a *daughter—existentially*—and I always would be. (161 f.)

By recalling this distinct memory, she vividly links her childhood self on an ordinary day at the kitchen table to the issue at the core of her quest.

## CHALLENGING THE SCRIPT

The narrator in *Motherhood* is confronted with a range of arguments for and against having children in her encounter with family, friends, and professionals such as physicians and psychologists. She recounts a conversation she had with her doctor when she had an abortion in her early twenties: the doctor tried to convince her to keep the baby (31). Her boyfriend Miles, who already has a daughter from a previous relationship who lives with her mother, leaves the decision in the narrative present to Sheila. He does not want another child. "If I want a child, we can have one, he said, *but you have to be sure*" (21). Several female friends think that she should attempt to conceive. In one instance, at the age of thirty-nine, she describes the prospect of wanting a child when it has become too late as an "anvil that will fall on my head to the laughter of all" (181). Somewhat contradictorily, though, she also comments: "I have always feared that I would regret having had one [child], more than regret *not* having" (189).

The book delivers a range of statements and rhetorical questions that emerge as challenging at the beginning of the twenty-first century when women in modern western societies have obtained an unparalleled level of freedom of choice concerning reproduction. She writes, for example:

There is something threatening about a woman who is not occupied with children. There is something at-loose-ends feeling about such a woman. What is she going to do instead? What sort of trouble will she make? (32)

What is a woman—who is not a mother—doing that is more important than mothering? Is it possible to even say such a thing—that there is anything more important for a woman to do than mother? (134)

And I don't want 'not a mother' to be part of who I am—for my identity to be the negative of someone else's positive identity. (157)

The hardest thing is actually *not* to be a mother—to refuse to be a mother to anyone. To not be a mother is the most difficult thing of all. (168 f.)

Sheila refers to the woman who has children as "the normal sort of woman" (22), indicating her awareness of a cultural script that she wishes to challenge. The narrative shifts between positions of acceptance and dispute, thus demonstrating how deep the discourse of motherhood and "normality" is embedded in thinking and practice. This is even more convincingly demonstrated by the narrator's meticulous effort to openly attend to her own feelings and observations in every detail.

In a review of the Swedish translation of *Motherhood*, the feminist critic Nina Björk (2018) critically notes that the book conveys "an absolute opposition between freedom and motherhood, and that freedom from such a relationship is a prerequisite for creative work."[2] To be seriously dedicated to creative work is incompatible with motherhood and mothering, in her reading of Heti. Björk draws attention to the fact that the freedom of choice that Heti describes is historically unique: today, many women can independently choose whether or not to have children. Björk's critique highlights differences not only in existential perspectives but also in social and political conditions. Sweden is a country with a comparatively generous and flexible child-care system which allows parents to continue their professional careers, and it is more or less taken for granted that women return to working life after their parental leave. From Sheila's Canadian middle-class perspective, she conveys the impression that her female friends seem to expect to lose their autonomy and professional position when having children, and that once they become mothers, they dedicate the major part of their time to motherhood. This is a reminder that class and economic demands shape reality as well as expectations related to motherhood. For Sheila, professional life seems impossible to combine with mothering, and as Alexandra Schwartz (2018) concludes in a review, the heart of the matter here is the act of writing: "A mother must make herself always available. A writer needs to shut the door."

The loss of a previous independent life is at the core of Rachel Cusk's narrative. She first notices this when she enters her home together with the baby: "It is only when I walk through the front door to my house that I realise things have changed. It is as if I have come to the house of

[2] All translations from Swedish are our own.

someone who has just died, someone I loved, someone I can't believe has gone" (56).

The writer she used to be is no longer. But her way of approaching motherhood is by reading what others have written on the subject. She is given manuals by medical staff during her pregnancy but gets no help from the patronizing advice which tells her that the baby will get liver damage if she eats paté or that she must stay away from cats if she does not want a baby with toxoplasmosis. The single topic, child birth, where Cusk really wants to be informed, is the only one where the manuals are less specific. When the baby is born Cusk has problems breastfeeding and turns to the manuals only to meet pictures of beautiful mothers who breastfeed their babies. Her difficulties are not reflected in the manuals where all mothers seem to be happy and content. This makes her feel even more lonely and inadequate. The focus on the *I* reinforces this sense of isolation. A partner, a man, is briefly mentioned, but Cusk stands alone as a mother. Becoming a mother is a transition from the known, the person she used to be, to an unfamiliar new world where she has to maneuver on her own. This is further underlined in the way she distances herself from others; she reads manuals on her own and she never reaches out to other mothers.

Everyday life is portrayed as claustrophobic, with Cusk and the baby alone in an apartment: "I have given up my membership of the world I used to live in," she writes in a chapter called "Hell's Kitchen." She describes how hard it is to respond to the baby's needs which always seem to be changing. As the baby grows she transforms from being "a ruck-sack" to an "escaped zoo animal" (143). The choice of words does not adhere to the way a loving mother is expected to describe her child, and Cusk's seemingly careless approach to her baby fueled criticism. When the baby starts to crawl Cusk is even more afraid to leave home since she fears what might happen. She feels increasingly trapped in the apartment and tries to figure out how she can get help. A nanny would be perfect but is a possibility only for the wealthy. The outer world enters her narrative when she hires immigrant women to look after the baby. The focus, however, is still on the *I* and there is a troubling distance in the way Cusk talks about these underprivileged women. The attention is on her feelings and that she cannot stop thinking about the baby after having left her at home: "I couldn't fit my world into a space carved, as it seemed to me, from my daughter's own flesh" (163). Even if she buys herself time it is impossible to retrieve her old self.

Cusk's earlier life and identity as a writer is incompatible with motherhood. Even if she manages to get time of her own she cannot use it. The
thought of the baby stands in the way. There is, however, one way in
which motherhood connects to her previous life. She reads differently,
which changes her outlook on literary texts: "Reading books to my daughter revives my appetite for expression. I read books that I have read before,
books that I love, and when I do I find them changed [...]. Could it be
true that one has to experience in order to understand? I have always
denied this idea, and yet of motherhood, for me at least, it seems to be the
case" (128). Cusk puts literary texts in dialogue with her narrative.
Rereading Coleridge's poem "Frost at Midnight" she discovers that she
has never before noticed the baby who is peacefully sleeping. She now
perceives how Coleridge captures a moment in this poem, together with
his infant, and how "his love finds a voice." Having experienced motherhood, Cusk reads the poem with a different attention. A connection is
after all established between herself as mother and her previous self.

Correspondingly, Sheila Heti describes a life dedicated to writing, publishing, and related activities: readings, travels to book events, talking to
people about issues that transform into literature. To this writer, the very
exercise of attention appears to be added to the list of reasons not to have
children.

## THE MATRILINEAL NARRATIVE

Both Rachel Cusk and Sheila Heti depict the modern woman as in many
ways self-reliant and autonomous. Both narratives, however, recognize the
maternal lineage, albeit in different ways. As Jo Malin has noted, in autobiographical writing the mother figure is often "embedded in a complex,
narrated relationship between mother and child" (Malin 2000, 2 f.).

With Heti, the extent to which her book is permeated with the relationship between mother and daughter is striking. The impact of this complicated relationship on Heti's indecision concerning motherhood has been
thoroughly examined by Gretchen Shirm (2022) from a psychoanalytical
perspective related to Melanie Klein's ideas about motherhood. Sheila
broods on her social responsibility as a complicating factor: her family are
Hungarian Jews, her grandmother experienced the Holocaust, and several
members of the family were murdered in Auschwitz. Families were
destroyed, and consequently reproduction is often seen as a moral obliga-
tion. Shirm reads this account as a "testimony" of an inherited trauma of

double consequence for Heti: "She's inviting us to draw a comparison between the personal and the public, and their respective effects on the individuals who experienced them." Three generations are in different ways affected by the "intergenerational trauma" (Shirm 2022, 15, 12).

Sheila's mother left Hungary (and her own mother) to get married in Canada. She was a trained physician and spent long periods working away from home when Sheila was a child. Early in the book, she recounts that she grew up with a mother who always cried and that she as a child was convinced that she was to blame for her mother's sadness (15). The memory still afflicts her. Her mother dedicated herself to her work and neglected her children who were raised by their father. From childhood, Sheila carries with her the image of what defines a mother, making it tangible by imaginatively placing her on a chair in a room of her own: "That is what a mother does: she sits in her room and works hard" (40).

The importance of the mother-daughter relationship is underscored by the fact that a significant part of the agony around motherhood seems to stem from the constantly negative attitude transmitted by Sheila's mother: that the children were a burden, that when they arrived her husband's love was transferred from her to them (82), and that work was more important than the children. Her mother's constant dissatisfaction makes the child Sheila draw the conclusion that it is her fault, that something is wrong with her (80). Her mother's grief has been transmitted to her, creating a life-long pain (143 f.). That the complicated relationship has an impact on her approach to motherhood is obvious: "Or maybe I feel betrayed by my mother, for not devoting herself to me and creating whatever loving memories must be created in a child to make her want to repeat the process again" (128).

The absent mother is notable also in Cusk's writing. She is mentioned, but mother and daughter do not seem to have a close relationship. When Cusk describes her fear of giving birth, her mother only replies that she should take any drug that they offer her during labor. This only reinforces the daughter's fear. The mother does not support her, and Cusk concludes that mothers today are on their own. This explains why child-care manuals play such an important role in the narrative. There is no generation of previous mothers to turn to.

The absent mother in Heti's book gradually becomes more visible during the course of the narrative. The narrative emerges as a process of reconciliation which is completed when Sheila sends her manuscript to her mother and receives a loving response. Gretchen Shirm (2022) describes this exchange from her psychoanalytical perspective as "a degree of reparation" (34). Sheila is finally to some extent at peace with her child-free life, which incidentally mirrors her childhood definition of what a mother does: "she sits in her room and works hard."

The acts of identification with and recognition from her mother seem to be determinative in finding an answer to the overriding question in *Motherhood*, and the book is a significant example of the matrilineal narrative that according to Yi-Lin Yu signifies much contemporary literature by women writers. Motherhood exists in a web of connections between generations. In order to understand these connections, the narratives explore the complicated bonds that continue to influence new generations. Yu defines matrilineal narratives in accordance with Tess Cosslett: "A 'matrilineal' narrative I define as one which either tells the stories of several generations of women at once, or which shows how the identity of a central character is crucially formed by her female ancestors" (Cosslett 1996, 7; Yu 2005, 2). Sheila revisits not only her mother but also her grandmother, in an attempt to come to grips with her understanding of motherhood. However, her exploration of the meaning of motherhood is characterized by consistent loyalty to her own perception, her own "exercise of attention" that contributes, as Moi formulates it in her Knausgaard analysis, to "create a world" (2017b). It is the protagonist's point of view, her field of vision, that is the starting point for the comprehensive contemplation on motherhood.

This also applies to Cusk's approach. She describes her experience of motherhood with no attempt to adjust it to the expected story of motherhood as a self-fulfilling practice. She takes care of and loves her baby, but she finds the endless daily chores exhausting, frustrating, and boring. This sets her apart from other mothers. When her family moves out of London to a university town, she notices that men are nowhere to be seen, but that she is surrounded by mothers. Cusk observes them, many older than herself, and they are everywhere with their small children. She does not approach them but sets herself apart as an observer. To her, life in the small town soon feels like a prison sentence, but she understands why it attracts mothers: "Its residential recesses were 'geared' to the good mother. This, I came to understand, was why so many mothers lived here. Here you could be free from the torments and temptations of life on the outside" (172). To Cusk, it only reminds her of the life she has lost. A health visitor advises her to join a toddlers group and she describes the event:

The organiser was bringing out cups and saucers which clattered loudly in her shaking hands. [...] She went about the room, bending discreetly towards the groups of talking women. *Coffee*, she mouthed to each one in a stage whisper, as if she were interrupting important meetings. Nearby, Cordelia's mother was discussing Cordelia's proclivities. Whenever she sees a black person, she said fondly, she just bursts into tears! It's quite embarrassing really, she added above the laughters of the others. She's obviously, you know, *a bit frightened*. They nodded their heads sympathetically, hands over their smiling mouths. *Coffee?* whispered the organiser next to my ear. (176 f.)

Cusk observes the interaction between the mothers which she does not take part in. This perspective reinforces the impression that she has nothing in common with the other mothers. Cusk is a writer, not a mother who adheres to the script of the good mother. She cannot devote herself to the baby in a self-effacing way and she cannot compromise on her intellectual integrity. This explains why *A Life's Work* challenged established norms on motherhood and stirred so much anger.

## SCRUTINIZING MOTHERHOOD

An important characteristic of both narratives discussed here is the astute and carefully described recognition of feelings of ambivalence and frustration. All kinds of irrational and unpleasant feelings are exposed. Sheila grieves the loss of friends who have children, being the one left behind. Cusk grieves the loss of the self she used to be. Both writers delve into their own emotional reactions to remarks, advice, or behavior among friends and family. The style connects to reality in a similar way as that which Moi observes in Knausgaard—a writing with a "capacity to convey reality," committed to "*attention*" ( Moi 2017b). As Moi underscores, such an endeavor involves both reader and writer:

But this means that the reader has to be willing to look, to examine her own world in the light of the writer's or the critic's invitation. For their part, the critic and the writer have to try to describe what they see as fully as possible. In so doing, they will necessarily reveal who they are, by which I mean they will reveal the specific nature of their own capacity for attention, at the same time as they say something about the world. (Moi 2017b)

This might help to explain the intense reactions triggered by the works on motherhood. The subject is apt to engage readers on a personal level as mothers or children, as having experienced complicated or non-existent relationships: experienced loss, grief, satisfaction or happiness. In our interpretation, the response is to a certain extent explained by the writers' ability to narrate reality, to engage themselves and the reader through careful attention to their perception of everyday life and its connection to existential questions (cf. Moi 2017b).

Furthermore, both texts illustrate simultaneously the individualization in modern society and the impossibility of making decisions about motherhood entirely on one's own. A recurrent point of reference is the human environment, indicating the dependence on social and emotional relations, and a timeline before and beyond the self.

As previously stated, motherhood is still a contested field. On Mother's Day in 2021 a young critic, Greta Thurfjell (2021), published an essay in a major Swedish newspaper, relating how when she was pregnant she was fed with horror stories about child birth and life with a baby to the extent that she felt relieved about how smooth everything turned out to be for her as a mother. She argued that it is time to balance all the dark stories with more positive ones.

Thurfjell was inspired by Elizabeth Bruenig's article "I Became a Mother at 25, and I'm Not Sorry I Didn't Wait," published on Mother's Day in *The New York Times* (Bruenig 2021). Bruenig had her first child in the midst of trying to launch herself as a journalist. There is a huge difference in how she experienced motherhood compared to Rachel Cusk. To Bruenig, the daily care of the baby was a relief "[f]or this member of a generation famously beset by anxiety." In Cusk's narrative there is an unbridgeable gap between the I, the self she wants to retain, and being a mother. This gap is never reconciled. Cusk explores motherhood, but this does not change the self in the text. Not so with Bruenig: "You never know who you are, because you are always changing." In her article Elizabeth Bruenig refers to Sheila Heti's book and describes the narrator as "a cynical writer contemplating whether to have kids before it's too late." Bruenig implies that Heti is too self-absorbed.

Elizabeth Bruenig's and Greta Thurfjell's articles show a generational difference, a sign that career and motherhood are no longer completely incompatible. They were both born in the 1990s. Moreover, the work of mothers is being reevaluated. Cusk disparages this work: "It erodes your self-esteem and your membership of the adult world" (13 f.). To Bruenig, motherhood has a positive impact on her professional life. Cusk's narrative stirred aggravation, but Bruenig's article also elicited reactions. Being both a young mother and a successful journalist, she was criticized for speaking from a white, privileged position, giving the impression that women can have it all. Nonetheless, Greta Thurfjell and Elizabeth Bruenig challenge the notion advanced by Cusk and Heti that being a mother and a writer is not compatible.

Sheila chooses not to become a mother. Whatever reasons women have for making that decision, it clearly challenges cultural scripts. "It makes me furious that 'voluntary' childlessness is still so often described as a project of self-realization, when in fact it contains an immense amount of more complicated issues," concludes the Swedish writer Annina Rabe (2013, 70). The works discussed here bring forward a similar viewpoint by highlighting a wide variety of aspects of motherhood and mothering— encompassing the personal and the political, the individual and the collective. For Sheila in *Motherhood*, the dichotomy between freedom and motherhood is all but fixed, ruling out the possibility of combining the two. On an existential level, however, the narrative is permeated with ambivalence: "On the one hand, the joy of children. On the other hand, the misery of them. On the one hand, the freedom of not having children. On the other hand, the loss of never having had them—but what is there to lose?" (21).

> Where are the texts in which "the voice of the mother" is not embedded in a daughter's story but is written by the mother herself? Why has this direct authorization of the mother's narrative and the sound of the mother's voice been foregrounded by the story of the daughter in women's autobiographies and the feminist theoretical discussion of women's autobiographies? (Malin 2000, 91)

Jo Malin's call was published two decades ago in her book *The Voice of the Mother: Embedded Maternal Narratives in Twentieth-Century Women's Autobiographies*. The works discussed here mirror the expanding range of theoretical and empirical reflection that has characterized research and literature about motherhood in recent decades. Today, the inquiry into motherhood merges the private and political, encompassing areas such as class, ethnicity, work, family, and home (Podnieks and O'Reilly 2010, Rye et al. 2018). Accordingly, Rachel Cusk and Sheila Heti refer to professional and family life, sex, reproduction, child care, gender, and money. They reveal to what extent motherhood is not an isolated question, but a concern for society at large.

To learn to see is to learn a language, concludes Toril Moi (2017a, 26). The works discussed here belong to a compelling genre of life writing where the careful attention to everyday life and personal thought deepens the interconnection between the self and the world. With their sharp and sensitive reflections, both *Motherhood* and *A Life's Work* recognize the complexity of a question that will remain important.

## References

Badinter, Élisabeth. 2011. *How Modern Motherhood Undermines the Status of Women*, translated by Adriana Hunter, New York: Metropolitan Books.

Björk, Nina. 2018. Sheila Heti har brännande funderingar i Moderskap, *Dagens Nyheter*, September 7.

Bruenig, Elizabeth. 2021. I Became a Mother at 25, and I'm Not Sorry I Didn't Wait, *The New York Times*, May 7.

Cosslett, Tess. 1996. Feminism, Matrilinealism, and the 'House of Women' in Contemporary Women's Fiction. *Journal of Gender Studies* 5 (1): 7–17.

Cusk, Rachel. 2008. (first published in 2001). *A Life's Work*. London: Faber and Faber.

DiQuinzio, Patrice. 1999. *The Impossibility of Motherhood: Feminism, Individualism, and the Problem of Mothering*. New York and London: Routledge.

Feigel, Lara. 2018. Motherhood by Sheila Heti Review – To Breed or not to Breed? *The Guardian*, June 6.

Heti, Sheila. 2018. *Motherhood*. London: Harvill Secker.

Malin, Jo. 2000. *The Voice of the Mother: Embedded Maternal Narratives in Twentieth-Century Women's Autobiographies*. Carbondale and Edwardsville: Sothern Illinois University Press.

Merkin, Daphne. 2021. A Very Lonely Business, *The New York Review of Books*, February 11, 2021: 27–29.

Miller, Tina. 2005. *Making Sense of Motherhood: A Narrative Approach*. Cambridge: Cambridge University Press.

Moi, Toril. 2017a. *Språk och uppmärksamhet*, translated by Alva Dahl, Stockholm: Faethon.

———. 2017b. Describing My Struggle, *The Point Magazine* online December 27.

Podnieks, Elizabeth, and Andrea O'Reilly. 2010. Maternal Literatures in Text and Tradition: Daughter-Centric, Matrilineal, and Matrifocal Perspectives. In *Textual Mothers/Maternal Texts: Motherhood in Contemporary Women's Literatures*, ed. Elizabeth Podnieks and Andrea O'Reilly, 1–27. Waterloo, ON: Wilfrid Laurier University Press.

Rabe, Annina. 2013. Ingen rättighet eller skyldighet. In *Ingens mamma. Tolv kvinnor om barnfrihet*, ed. Josefine Adolfsson, 66–78. Stockholm: Atlas.

Rye, Gill, Victoria Browne, Adalgisa Giorgio, Emily Jeremiah, and Abigail Lee Six, eds. 2018. *Motherhood in Literature and Culture: Interdisciplinary Perspectives from Europe.* New York and London: Routledge.

Schwartz, Alexandra. 2018. Sheila Heti wrestles with a big decision in 'Motherhood'. *The New Yorker*, May 7.

Shirm, Gretchen. 2022. Sheila Heti, Melanie Klein and *Motherhood*. *Critique: Studies in Contemporary Fiction*. Published online January 3. https://www.tandfonline.com/doi/full/10.1080/00111619.2021.2024128  (accessed February 16, 2022).

Thurfjell, Greta. 2021. Att bli mamma var inte alls så jobbigt som de sa. *Dagens Nyheter*, May 30.

Yu, Yi-Lin. 2005. *Mother, She Wrote: Matrilineal Narratives in Contemporary Women's Writing.* New York: Peter Lang.

# CHAPTER 9

# A Plea for Motherhood: Mothering and Writing in Contemporary Norwegian Literature

## Christine Hamm

While mothers and motherhood have been thematized in Norwegian literature since the nineteenth century, mothering emerged as a dominant

This publication has received funding from the European Union's Horizon 2020 research and innovation programme under grant agreement No 952366, and from the Centre for Gender Research and the Department of Literature at Uppsala University.

C. Hamm (✉)
Department of Linguistic, Literary and Aesthetic Studies, University of Bergen, Bergen, Norway
e-mail: christine.hamm@uib.no

H. Wahlström Henriksson et al. (eds.), *Narratives of Motherhood and Mothering in Fiction and Life Writing*, Palgrave Macmillan Studies in Family and Intimate Life, https://doi.org/10.1007/978-3-031-17211-3_9

theme just after the turn of the last century.[1] In 2018, four well-established authors were among those who published novels with mothers as narrators and protagonists. Kjersti Annesdatter Skomsvold's novel *Barnet* [The child, 2018][2] gives voice to a woman who has just given birth to her second child. The narrator describes the life-changing experience of giving birth and taking care of another human being, and she explores how she ended up having children at this point in her life. Heidi Furre published *Dyret* [The animal, 2018], a novel about a young woman who gets pregnant, gives birth and learns to take care of her baby in the first weeks of its life. In *Rase* [Rage, 2018], Monica Isakstuen explores a young writer's effort to deal with her situation as a mother to three small children. She finds herself becoming angry in a way she has never experienced before. Inger Bråtveit's novel *Dette er også vatn* [This is also water, 2018] tells the story of a woman who is forced into the position of a single mother of three children after her husband falls ill. She is also a writer who needs time for herself. Earlier, she had been a passionate swimmer, and she here compares both mothering and writing to moving long distances through water.[3]

Why did Skomsvold, Furre, Isakstuen and Bråtveit all choose to write texts about mothering in 2018? In the following sections, I will show that the decision to mother is the major issue for the narrators in all four

---

[1] In the first ten years of the twenty-first century, Norwegian critics nevertheless ignored the subject of mothering in literature. I have earlier commented on the reception of novels dealing with motherhood that had appeared right after the millennium shift, such as Trude Marstein's *Plutselig høre noen åpne en dør* [Suddenly hearing someone open a door, 2000] and Vigdis Hjorth's *Hva er det med mor* [What is happening with mother, 2000]. I argued that literary critics at that time avoided reading those novels as texts about mothering, since they obviously thought that would lessen the novels' aesthetic value (Hamm 2013). The situation has now changed, and critics seem no longer to have problems with motherhood as a subject.

[2] All translations of Norwegian titles and texts in this chapter are my own.

[3] All four authors had written several acclaimed novels by 2018, and most of them had won prizes. Skomsvold was given the Tarjei Vesaas prize for new writers and shortlisted for the IMPAC Dublin Literary Award in 2009, for her first novel *Jo fortere jeg går, jo mindre er jeg* [The faster I walk, the smaller I am]. Isakstuen's breakthrough novel *Vær snill med dyrene* [Be kind to the animals, 2016] was awarded with the prestigious Bragepris [Brage Prize] for literature in Norway. Bråtveit's *Siss og Unn* in 2008 gained her a nomination for the Kritikerprisen [The Critics' Prize]. She also was given the Nynorsk prize for literature and won a Bjørnson grant.

novels. I interpret the effort of the narrators to accept—and even defend—the decision they have made to be mothers in connection with the setting of the novels: contemporary Norway. This setting means that the narrators live in a country where women are strongly encouraged to have professional careers and where educated writers are familiar with the dangers of patriarchal ideology and its premise that all women would want to mother. To be a mother can to some women with professional careers even feel as a betrayal of feminist politics in a country with the declared wish to promote gender equality on all fields. The choice to become a mother in 2018, therefore, seems to demand an explanation, even a defense.

My argument is that the four Norwegian novels can be read as what I call "pleas for motherhood"—pleas that the narrators perform in order to understand and accept themselves. Since the 1970s, the Norwegian government has encouraged both women and men to be employed, and a major effort has been made to secure enough daycare-places for children.[4] In 2016, Norway became the first country to have a "Gender Equality Ombud," something that reflects the country's long-lasting and outspoken effort to guarantee the same rights for women and men. A secure relation to the working sphere is crucial for receiving all benefits in the welfare-state, including a total of 48 weeks of paid leave from work for either of the parents when they have a child.[5] In this way, the state promotes the idea that having a professional career and secure employment is the first task for a woman to achieve, while motherhood is still taken for granted.

I read the novels as a reaction to the place motherhood has in the Norwegian state-supported thinking about gender equality. My analysis reveals the narratives in the novels of the four writers as well-designed defenses against something the protagonists seem to feel accused of. This "something" is their own lack of support of earlier feminist positions, as

---

[4] Norway's newest act relating to equality and prohibition against discrimination from 2018 ("Lov om likestilling og forbud mot diskriminering") ensures that female employees receive the same treatment, work security, income and status as men. Further, the act is meant to prevent discrimination based on ethnicity, national origin, descent, skin color, language, religion or belief. Lov om likestilling og forbud mot diskriminering (likestillings- og diskrimineringsloven) - Lovdata (accessed March 25, 2022).

[5] Fifteen weeks must be taken by the father, which is regulated by the "Lov om folketrygd, part V. Lov om folketrygd (folketrygdloven) - II. Foreldrepenger - Lovdata (accessed March 25, 2022)

represented in their careers as successful writers. Hence, the theme of writing plays an important role in the novels; in the analysis I shall clarify how the novels deal with tensions and links between mothering and writing.

## THE CHOICE OF GENRE: NOVELS OR MOTHERHOOD MEMOIRS?

I argue that the four authors share the project of exploring Norwegian women's felt need to defend their choice to become mothers. Further, I will emphasize that they chose to write novels, meaning complex and aesthetically refined works of art. The choice of genre can be explained by the complexity of the issue of motherhood and its relation both to feminism and to patriarchal ideology. The question of genre became relevant already when the novels first appeared. In an article in *Klassekampen*'s book magazine on February 24 the same year, literary critic Silje Bekeng-Flemmen wondered why there were so few novels on mothering on the market. When looking for books dealing with the subject during her own pregnancy, she found that there was a vast amount of self-help material and non-fiction books on pregnancy and mothering in Norwegian bookstores, but, she claimed, she could not find "serious fiction" on the subject (Bekeng-Flemmen 2018). When this kind of literature appeared later that year, the authors of the novels, who all recently had undergone pregnancy and childbirth, were accordingly asked if they had experienced the same need for such literature as Bekeng-Flemmen.

As it turned out, the four authors differed in their answers. In an interview with journalist and book reviewer Astrid Hygen Meyer on July 23, Heidi Furre said, as the mother of a newborn, she went "to find a sort of confirmation in literature" ("for å finne en slags bekreftelse i litteraturen"). She said she was looking for a text that could grasp the difficulty and complexity of the experience she went through. The same journalist also interviewed Kjersti Annesdatter Skomsvold, who however explained that she did not look for books by others, but that she herself strongly felt the need to write about the experience of being a mother, and wanted to explore her anxiety and her fears (Meyer 2018).

The fact that all four authors themselves were mothers when they started writing about mothering aroused suspicions that they were using writing to "make sense of motherhood," a formulation used by sociologist Tina Miller in her classical narrative approach (Miller 2005). In the eyes of Norwegian critics, it seems, this would have lessened the aesthetic quality of the books and would have made their status as novels problematic. Norwegian critics like Frode Helmich Pedersen classified the four books accordingly,[6] claiming in a comment in *Dagbladet* on August 7, 2018, that "novels" about mothering are made possible by the ongoing tendency in Scandinavian literature to write "virkelighetslitteratur" [reality literature] (Pedersen 2018).[7] As he saw it, this trend encourages white middle-class writers to deal with private problems in public. Without having studied the specific texts any closer, Pedersen seemed to imagine that novels about mothering that appeared in the year 2018 were what researchers elsewhere called "momoirs," that is, motherhood memoirs.[8]

The Norwegian texts would then fit well with the global tendency of exploring motherhood through autobiographical narratives (two of the best-known examples in English-language literature are Rachel Cusk's *A Life's Work* [2001] and Sheila Heti's *Motherhood* [2018]).[9] Seen in this way, the novels would belong to a genre that has in the past provoked ambivalent reactions, as Joanne Frye and Andrea O'Reilly described in their respective articles in *Textual Mothers/Maternal Texts* (2010). According to O'Reilly, motherhood memoirs as well as "Mommy-Lit" are mainly characterized by a writer's effort to cope with the challenging situation of being a mother as honestly as possible (2010, 203). While one should welcome the attention devoted to motherhood, mothering and the related challenges (Frye 2010, 187), the problem is that overarching ideologies governing images of mothers in most cases are reproduced; for instance, the ideology that a mother should be totally devoted to her children and should think more about her children than her work, and that men and women in principle develop different attitudes toward their children. This, at least, is how Ivana Brown (2006) and Andrea O'Reilly (2010) concluded their investigations into the genre. They argued that motherhood memoirs are part of what Susan Douglas and Meredith Michaels called the "New Momism" (2004), an ideology which includes

---

[6] Another critic was Endre Ruset, who claimed that the four Norwegian novels were too much alike and therefore aesthetically weak (Ruset 2018).

[7] "Virkelighetslitteratur" is a label for novels written after the year 2000 in which the writers and their close friends and family are among the protagonists. The most famous examples of this trend in Norwegian literature are Karl Ove Knausgård's series of six novels *Min kamp* [My struggle, 2009–2011] and Vigdis Hjorth's novel *Arv og miljø* [translated into *Wills and Testaments*, 2016].

[8] The genre is also called the "Mommy memoir" (Brown 2006) or the "Maternal memoir" (Frye 2010).

[9] Andrea O'Reilly is among those who have commented on this global trend (O'Reilly 2010). See also Fahlgren and Williams, Chap. 8 this volume.

the idea that career women can freely choose to give up their paid work and "return" to their homes and feel like better humans for making that shift.

However, the novels written by Skomsvold, Furre, Isakstuen and Bråtveit in 2018 are in fact not motherhood memoirs. In the following, my point of departure is the label "novels" attached to the texts. My analysis pays attention to the aesthetic form the writers have chosen in each case, and asks what the genre of the novel offers to the authors' projects of bringing out the situation of Norwegian mothers. It will become clear that *Barnet* and *Dyret* develop the idea that motherhood lets a woman become engaged with other human beings, and that for the protagonists writing a novel is, it seems, part of this engagement. *Rase* and *Dette er også vatn*, on the other hand, stress the fact that becoming a mother demands that a woman accept the circumstances and let go of control. Writing an aesthetic text enables the narrators of these two novels to accept mothering as meaningful in the 2010s.[10] Because the narrators in the novels do not take the meaning and the importance of motherhood for granted, the novels do not support what Sharon Hays has called "intensive mothering" (Hays 1996) nor the illusion of a free choice for women that is typical for "New Momism" (O'Reilly 2010). Instead, deprived of a free life with enough time for both work and relationships with other adults, the women in the novels somehow seem to feel the need to defend the choice to become a mother in the first place. When describing their experience of mothering, they try to formulate their reasons for choosing childbirth and mothering despite their awareness of patriarchy and its motherhood discourse. The genre of the novel enables the authors to perform serious investigations into motherhood, both as a part of patriarchal ideology and as an issue for feminist critique fueled by individualism.

## Mothering and Writing as Opening to the World: Skomsvold's *Barnet* and Furre's *Dyret*

At a first glance, Kjersti Annesdatter Skomsvold's novel *Barnet* comes very close to a piece of life-writing. The text has no chapters and contains a seemingly arbitrarily collected heap of fragments. A closer look reveals that the text is divided into three parts by two blank pages. The first part

---

[10] The challenge for women to relate to the question of motherhood and the lack of a convincing discourse on the subject is well addressed in Patrice DiQuinzio's *The Impossibility of Motherhood* (1999).

contains the thoughts and reflections of the mother/writer-narrator during the second week of her baby daughter's life (her second child), while the second part includes reflections when the daughter is about six weeks. The third part starts with the mother telling her daughter that she is now three months old. While one first gets the impression that the mother is talking directly to her second child while staying at home with her, it turns out that she is writing down her thoughts. The text is revealed as a mask of a direct and spontaneous conversation.

Skomsvold's narrator, a professional writer, asks herself what status writing has in her life after she gives birth. She knows very well that, at some earlier point, she had thought to not be part of this world, that she thought she was only living in her texts. The narrator compares herself to the artist Agnes Martin, who after a while did not want to live with her lovers or her children. Skomsvold found she had a similar project: "I also wanted to write with my back against the world, I was afraid to do something else, and I could have chosen like she did, I could have asked God to not get pregnant. But then I just have this one life."[11] As becomes clear in *Barnet*, the narrator is conscious about the choice of motherhood as excluding the possibility of living "with her back against the world" (as did Martin). Mothering is seen as being opposed to writing, as something that would pull the writer into this world.

After the birth of her first child, the narrator had thought she might find a new language. She was expecting that something refreshingly new would start. However, it turned out that she could not write about the experience of having given birth at all. Rather, she relates how she went through a crisis that stole her words from her (Skomsvold 2018, 26). Having given birth to her second child, she therefore forces herself to write everything down; she needs to regain the words she lost two years ago.

She interprets her need to write as something that enables her to keep control over herself, something that paradoxically includes losing the very same control: "When I write, I decide who I am, but even when writing it is first when I give up protecting myself that I can recognize myself, when I get rid of the thought of what the whole thing should be, become, and

---

[11] Jeg ville også skrive med ryggen mot verden, jeg var livredd for å gjøre noe annet, og jeg kunne ha valgt som henne, jeg kunne ha bedt til Gud om å få slippe. Men så har jeg bare dette ene livet (Skomsvold 2018, 16).

it is just like that with love, too."[12] It seems as if the narrator needs the written text to find out who she is. She needs to reconcile her writing, her words and her motherhood.

Reconciliation includes her recounting why she became a mother in the first place, thereby finding words for that experience. After scribbling down how she met her husband, how long it took for her to let him be part of her life, she suddenly finds that the idea of having a child has entered her mind. Inspired by her husband's wish for a child, she visualizes her own childhood and recognizes that she is afraid of ending up alone, without a family: "I loved my family, and now I saw myself sitting in the kitchen alone, for the rest of my life. That was impossible. That should not happen. We need to have children, I said."[13] As becomes clear, writing the novel enables the mother-narrator to understand herself and her decisions. She finds an explanation for why she, a writer who had so much time for herself and who thought she did not need what she calls "the world" (prosaic everyday routines and other people to care for and relate to), suddenly longed for it, wanted to be part of it, as if she was about to lose it.

The importance of finding a language for making sense of the experience of motherhood is also stressed in Heidi Furre's novel *Dyret*. Its structure—the numbering of the chapters—mirrors the time from the moment a young woman in her late twenties gets pregnant, to the point when her daughter is six weeks old (chapters 40 + 6, explained below). However, much like Skomsvold's book, the text at first looks more like a piece of life-writing than a novel. It takes some time for the reader to become aware of the meaning of the structure; in fact, this realization happens only when she learns about the narrator's pregnancy and her need to keep track of the development of the fetus from week to week with the help of an app. When the narrator gives birth and the chapters start afresh from 0 and onward, it is finally confirmed that the chapters follow the age of the child, first in the womb, then outside of it.

The short, episodically told chapters tell us that the narrator first lives together with her friend Henny. The women are close friends, but when the narrator becomes pregnant and subsequently a mother, they become

---

[12] I skrivingen bestemmer jeg selv hvem jeg er, men også der er det først idet jeg gir opp beskyttelsen, at det blir noe jeg kan kjenne meg igjen i, når jeg kommer løs fra tanken om hva det skal være, bli, og sånn er det med kjærligheten også (Skomsvold 2018, 44).

[13] Jeg elsket familien min, og nå så jeg for meg at jeg skulle sitte alene ved kjøkkenbordet resten av livet. Det gikk jo ikke. Det kunne ikke skje. Vi må få barn, sa jeg (Skomsvold 2018, 78).

estranged from each other. The last six chapters show the narrator in interaction with her little baby. The novel concludes with an epilogue, in which the narrator reflects on the famous picture of the drowned boy on the beach (Alan Kurdi, a three-year-old refugee from Syria). The narrator tells us that she does not know if having a child is important, but she knows that children matter and that adults are responsible for them: "I don't know if it is important to have children, to be a mother or a father. I only know that all children are our children."[14] Thus, at the end of the text, the focus has changed from the perspective of the mother and the narrator's effort to find out about the relationship to her own child, to the perspective of children, and that they principally need to be taken care of.

Furre's novel concentrates less than Skomsvold's on the experience of raising a child; rather, it describes the process of pregnancy and, consequently, having to change one's life. As I see it, Furre's text explores how this change comes about, and how it somehow forms a parallel with what happens to the body (childbirth after pregnancy includes a splitting of the self from one into two). The narrator wants to find her own way, becoming aware of her own, separated body. She first clings to the idea that she will find out what to do somehow instinctively, in the same way that animals do (therefore the novel's title). At one time she feels that nature takes over her life: "Nature takes over, and me, I have walked around my whole life thinking of my body as a kind of tool, not the other way around."[15] The feeling of being no longer in control of her body, but being controlled by it, begins with the experience of nausea, as the narrator fights her way onto the bus to her job in a canteen, where she works with preparing food for about 100 persons. Nature has her also walking around with a big belly, something that needs to be hidden until she gets a permanent job offer. She manages to get one, cynically using the fact that her boss sends her sex texts for her own benefit. She threatens to send them to his wife, with the result that he offers her a permanent contract.

With the child developing in her body, the narrator's perspective on her life changes. Having been a student without a clear goal, a woman flirting

---

[14] Eg veit ikkje om det er viktig å ha eit barn, å vere ei mamma eller ein pappa. Eg veit berre at alle barn er våre (Furre 2018, 169).
[15] Naturen har innhenta meg, her har eg gått rundt heile livet og trudd at kroppen er mitt verktøy, ikkje motsett (Furre, 2018, 26).

with new men every evening and dancing with Henny, even tolerating harassment, she now enters a permanent relationship, finds an apartment for the new family and buys books about mothering and child rearing. Having come out of the experience of being controlled by the fetus and just being part of nature, she now controls her life with language and by recounting her life in an aesthetic text. She has turned into a responsible adult, having eyes not only for her own daughter Lux but also for all children. The plea for motherhood in this novel, then, is that when becoming a mother, a woman is forced to be a human being who has eyes for the life of others.

## Mothering and the Acceptance of the Everyday in Isakstuen's *Rase* and Bråtveit's *Dette er også vatn*

The narrator in Monica Isakstuen's novel *Rase* [Rage] is a writer who lives in a big house with a husband who is supporting her in the effort to combine children and work. She has a daughter from a former relationship and young twin sons. As soon becomes clear, the narrator suffers because she is frustrated with the situation in the family. Each day, she ends up screaming at the children and she is afraid of how far she might go in the end: "I am afraid of my hands."[16] The narrator tries to figure out how she got into the situation of having three children, and she asks herself, "How does one know when something starts? Are there clear moments that cut time into parts, one part before and one after?"[17] The narrator wonders who she is, because she cannot recognize herself anymore: "What kind of human being am I, really?"[18] She has an urgent need to confirm her identity, as if the situation of being a mother has forced her to accept someone else instead of herself.

As the narrator comes to learn, living with three children means having no time at all for herself or for discussing things with the man she loves. Everything is absorbed by daily duties. The narrator gets into a crisis and finally seeks the help of a therapist, who asks her to visualize scenes of her life. This explains why the novel is a collection of fragments, containing

---

[16] Jeg er redd for hendene mine (Isakstuen 2018, 21).

[17] Men hvordan vet man at noe begynner? Finnes slike klare øyeblikk som skjærer gjennom tiden og deler den i to, et før og et etter? (Isakstuen 2018, 16).

[18] Hva slags menneske er jeg egentlig? (Isakstuen 2018, 27).

scenes from her life with the children. Before she started therapy, the therapist had explained his method to her:

> Regarding the sessions lasting one hour, or sixty minutes, to be precise, they mainly meant that the patient closed her eyes and opened herself up for the thoughts to come, dreams or pieces of daily life, as he called it, loose fragments of thoughts or whatever drifted by, he said one could imagine being on a train and seeing how the landscape raced by fast [*raste*], and that one then should tell someone else what one observed on the trip.[19]

The fact that the therapist uses the verb "rase" (to race by) when describing what happens to the visualized scenes, and thus stresses the combination with the word for rage (the title of the book), is of course no coincidence. The reader is meant to see that the way the novel is told, with the fragments, is like the method used in the therapy of the person telling the story (= the narrator). However, the narrator in that way not only comments on what she sees (= she renders not only what has really happened), but what she thinks might possibly happen. In addition, she reflects on what she tells, as does the therapist in the novel. The therapist suggests, for instance, that one reason for the anger the narrator feels might be her fear of having to find out that she regrets her choice. He thinks she is afraid of finding out that she did not want the children after all.

The novel ends when the narrator sees that her children will develop and have a life independent of her. The last scene shows the narrator and her children at a performance, and one of her sons volunteers to get on stage and sing a song before the crowd. The narrator is astonished that he has the courage to do this; it is as if she only now gets to know him. She understands that she, wrongly, had thought of her children as things she owns, as things she would be fully responsible for. It is as if she only now recognizes that she does not own her son the way she thought she did, but that he is a separate human being. This understanding helps her to see that

---

[19] Når det gjaldt timene, klokketimer, presiserte han, gikk de stort sett ut på at den som ble behandlet lukket øynene og ga plass til det som kom, drømmer eller hverdagsrester, som han kalte det, løse tankefragmenter eller hva nå enn som fløt forbi, han sa man kunne forestille seg at man satt i en togkupe og at man, mens landskapet raste i vei på utsiden, skulle forsøke å formidle hva man så på togturen sin, til den man snakket med (Isakstuen 2018, 49).

what she does as a mother is not total destiny: "My words and hands are not the only things that form him. He is his own, he is free."[20] Isakstuen lets the narrator find out that mothering is important, but not everything. It is in fact rather dangerous if a woman demands too much of herself as a mother. Instead of subscribing to what Susan Douglas and Meredith Michaels have called the ideology of intensive mothering (2004, 6), the narrator on the contrary recognizes that she should accept that she can only reach so far. Telling the story, consciously using the device of ordering the sequences like therapeutic sessions, helps the narrator to work through her fear concerning mothering, and to realize that an explanation for mothering might not be so important. Rather, it is important to accept being a mother. The plea for motherhood in the novel turns out to be a plea for a kind of "ordinary" motherhood that differs from what Patrice DiQuinzio has called essential motherhood.[21] Isakstuen asks for the right to be a mother who gives just enough attention and care to her children; she claims the right to enjoy an everyday life with her husband, her friends and her work, as well as with her children.

Inger Bråtveit's novel *Dette er også vatn* [This is also water] is at first sight only loosely connected to the question of motherhood. However, a closer look reveals the book to be an exploration of the narrator's identity. The need for this exploration is caused by the desperate situation that she suddenly finds herself in, as a writer and a single mother with three children. Having a daughter by herself, who is one and a half years old at the beginning of the novel and five and a half at the end, she also takes care of two older stepsons who need her attention because her husband has fallen ill with Lyme disease. The consequence of his illness is that she has no time to write, and when the text jumps from one subject to another, it gives the impression of the author-protagonist losing control.

One of the main themes, as the title indicates, is water, and especially saltwater, which is found, for instance, in the fjord outside the house

---

[20] Mine ord og mine hender er ikke det eneste som former ham. Han er sin egen, han er fri (Isakstuen 2018, 223).

[21] In *The Impossibility of Motherhood*, DiQuinzio explains "essential motherhood" in this way: "Essential motherhood is an ideological formation that specifies the essential attributes of motherhood and articulates femininity in terms of motherhood so understood. [...] Essential motherhood construes women's motherhood as natural and inevitable. It requires women's exclusive and selfless attention to and care of children based on women's psychological and emotional capacities for empathy, awareness of the need for others, and self-sacrifice" (DiQuinzio 1999, xiii).

where the narrator grew up. The water that surrounds the narrator is associated both with her mother ("Vatnet er ei mor" [the water is a mother], *Dette er også vatn*, p. 15), or is even seen as being an alternative mother, surrounding the body of the narrator when she swims and dives, and in way gives birth to herself: "The sea is like velvet. The sea says now swim as far as you can."[22] But the water is also associated with mothering, not least at the moment when the narrator is swimming against the stream and sees it as a metaphor for just hanging in there, for not giving up on getting everything done, on tolerating pain due to pregnancy and mothering, day by day: "I swim through pelvic pain, mastitis, carpal tunnel syndrome, heart rates of your and my children, and I fall and swim like hell."[23] To keep on swimming in saltwater, against the forces of the wind and the cold, is like looking after children every day, preparing food, changing diapers and cleaning the house. One hopes one makes it.

At the same time, swimming is also associated with writing. Writing demands, as swimming does, that the writer opens herself up to the experience, and that she just goes on, even if she finds things she does not like: "I think that swimming is like writing and reading."[24] To write is to let scenes pass by, and the novel is built up accordingly of pieces of memory (of her father dying of cancer, of her sister being better than her at skiing and swimming, of her uncle and her grandmother working in the countryside when she was a child), of reflections on literature and historical events (stories by Tove Jansson, the Kursk submarine tragedy, the war in Serbia and Croatia), and of scenes from her present life (her journey to Sweden, her experience as a teacher). It is as if the reader is forced to dive through the text as the narrator does through her memories.

Because the narrator swims through her own thoughts, reflecting that action by associative writing, she finally manages to see that this is the meaning of mothering, like the meaning of swimming, and that there it is no other way to go on. She writes: "So what should one do? When one thinks and hopes one is right, but is wrong for a long time? One has to write. Administrate the writing through time and space. To swim into love, through hate, into ecstasy. I take charge and kick off, fall through

---

[22] Havet var som fløyel. Havet sa at no sym du så langt du kan (Bråtveit 2018, 18).
[23] Eg sym gjennom bekkenløysing, brystbetennelsar, karpaltunnelsyndrom, hjartefrekvensane til dine og mine barn, og eg fell og sym som berre faen (Bråtveit 2018, 33).
[24] Eg tenkjer at å symja liknar på å skriva og lesa (Bråtveit 2018, 31).

blue-green water, fold out and pull together."[25] Comparing mothering to swimming, however, poses the question of what happens when winter comes, and everything freezes to ice. The narrator asks: "What happens when one does not find a language to use? When language freezes over somehow, due to imagined responsibility, but when what we try to say is there, inside us, just beneath the ice?"[26]

Luckily, winter will turn into spring and summer. In the fifth and final part (the book follows the age of the daughter), the narrator and her family are on a holiday in a town close to Zagreb. It is very hot, and she is teaching her now five-year-old daughter how to swim. She is happy she can teach her daughter how to keep herself floating in the water. The narrator registers that the waves are coming and going: "The waves are coming in, and then pull out again slowly. It is as if the waves try to escape the sea."[27] In the same way that the waves come and go, motherhood has changed and is still the same. "You are my best friend, says my daughter, while I am thinking no, and answer yes."[28] This passage seems to tell us that the daughter is just fine, as fine as one can be. The narrator concludes by telling the readers that motherhood is something beautiful but that it needs to be performed each day in small pieces, just like writing. In establishing her plea for motherhood, she now thinks that one can find a kind of text about mothering in the sea, that the sea takes care of bits of memories and pictures and sounds that one can pick up from the bottom and find a place for in the daylight.

## THE PLEA FOR MOTHERHOOD IN NORWAY

Skomsvold shows with her novel how writing first excludes motherhood, then how motherhood excludes writing. In the end, however, it is writing that makes it acceptable for the protagonist to be a mother. At the same time, finding words for her mothering also means sharing her experience

---

[25] Så kva skal ein gjera? Om ein trur og håpar å ha rett, men i lange tider tek feil? Ein får skriva. Forvalta skrivinga gjennom tida og avstanden. Symja inn i kjærleiken, gjennom hatet mot ekstasen. Eg tek sats og fråspark, fell gjennom blågrønt vatn, faldar meg ut og klemmer meg samman (Bråtveit 2018, 33).

[26] For kva hender når med ikkje har språket å tala med? Når språket er frose fast av ulike årsaker og innbilt ansvar, men det me vil seia, finst der, i oss, like under isen? (Bråtveit 2018, 48).

[27] Bølgjene slår inn, for så å dra seg sakte ut og attende att. Det er som om bølgjene prøver å rømma frå havet (Bråtveit 2018, 161).

[28] Du er min beste venn, seier dotter mi, medan eg tenkjer nei og seier ja (Bråtveit 2018, 161).

with others. In Furre's novel, the narrator's recounting of having a child, even if it has not been planned, brings out how the experience of pregnancy turns a self-centered and lazy person into someone who takes responsibility not only for her own life and her child's life but also for others. Furre's narrator understands that she went through the illusion of being only a body, of being reduced to nature, before she finds her human voice and takes on responsibilities. In Isakstuen's novel, the narrator tries to deal with fears of harming her children. She is frustrated and angry, realizing that she is not living up to the ideal of a perfect mother. The collection of fragments containing episodes of her life is a kind of therapy, since it enables her to understand what is going on. She finds out that she does not own her children, that they also develop outside her influence. Similarly, the mother-narrator in Bråtveit's text needs the collection of memories, reflections and small essayistic pieces to find out who she is as a mother, daughter, niece and sister. She realizes that she must keep on swimming through her associations, through her thoughts, she must keep on struggling as mother as well as writer. Although the narrator never finds out why she mothers, the effect is nevertheless that the process is experienced as meaningful.

My analysis of the novels has shown how the four texts at first look very much like life-writing in that they (in part) come close to motherhood memoirs. Giving voice to narrators who are mothers simultaneously with giving interviews on their own situations as mothers, the Norwegian authors invite readers to approach the texts as pieces of autobiographical writing. However, a closer look shows that the texts are aesthetically refined, they use symbols and metaphors, and they are consciously structured. The authors reveal themselves as experienced writers of fiction who are using the genre of the novel to bring out challenges for mothers: some of the women in the novels must change, become someone different, and some of them must accept themselves and their situation.

Skomsvold, Furre, Isakstuen and Bråtveit let their narrators reflect on how they ended up having children, and on the fact that they chose motherhood. Precisely because they do not accept motherhood as something every woman necessarily must experience, they feel the need to account for why a woman nevertheless would want to become a mother and go on mothering. Writing helps the narrators understand their motivations for becoming mothers, while for them, writing in itself becomes part of being a mother.

Like in the US, Canada and the UK, expressions of New Momism are certainly also to be found in Norway. Especially in women's magazines and blogs, Norwegian women publish on mothering, and many women stress that motherhood was their free choice. However, there are also strong feminist voices criticizing this kind of ideology. As early as 2004, the feminist literary critic Toril Moi reacted harshly in her column in the newspaper *Morgenbladet* to what she saw as a "harping on motherhood" (Moi 2004). She claimed that the many pictures of mothers and their children in Norwegian papers would make it hard for women to see motherhood as something else than destiny, and that motherhood therefore could not be seen as something women were able to choose freely. Moi thought Norwegian women talking about their free choices were suffering from false consciousness and she appealed to women to fight against this thinking (Grov 2012).

When Moi wrote her critique, most Norwegian women in fact became mothers at some point. Some years later, however, the situation had changed. While Norwegian women on average gave birth to 1.98 children in the year 2009, they only had 1.62 children in 2017. The fall in the fertility rate alarmed the Prime Minister Erna Solberg (conservative party) so much that, in her traditional New Year's speech on January 1, 2019, she asked Norwegian women to choose motherhood. She no longer took it for granted that women would want to be mothers. But her speech was harshly criticized in the Norwegian press.[29] In a country that is proud of having gender equality as one of its core values, and of having most women in paid work, few Norwegians tolerate it when women are asked to become mothers. To appeal for motherhood is just not acceptable. My suggestion would therefore be that the plea for motherhood, which I have detected in the four novels discussed here, results from the narrators' (and, perhaps, the authors') felt need to defend motherhood against feminist attacks on motherhood and their felt need to problematize motherhood as taken for granted in contemporary Norway. The authors let their narrators investigate their own specific cases, why they have decided to become mothers, since they feel that convincing arguments for motherhood are no longer available in public discourse and on a general level.

While many previous Norwegian novels about mothers and motherhood have been devoted to debunking patriarchal ideals of motherhood, novels by women writers today also show a struggle with feminist

---

[29] For reactions to the speech, see, for instance, Benedicte Sørum's article in *Kilden*, January 29, 2019. https://kjonnsforskning.no/nb/2019/01/be-kvinner-fode-flere-barn-bryter-med-norsk-familiepolitikk-mener-forskere

expectations, as well as with individualistic ideologies. By using the genre of the novel, the writers discussed in this chapter bring out efforts to advocate motherhood in different ways. The texts are stressing the protagonists' ethical insights and artistic growth, while also insisting on the importance of acknowledging mothering as just another part of life.

## References

Bekeng-Flemmen, Silje. 2018. Ny i livet. *Klassekampen*, February 24.
Bråtveit, Inger. 2018. *Dette er også vatn*. Roman. Oslo: Forlaget oktober.
Brown, Ivana. 2006. Mommy Memoirs: Feminism, Gender and Motherhood in Popular Literature. *Journal of the Association for Research on Mothering* 8 (1 & 2): 200–212.
DiQuinzio, Patrice. 1999. *The Impossibility of Motherhood. Feminism, Individualism, and the Problem of Mothering*. New York and London: Routledge.
Douglas, Susan, and Meredith Michaels. 2004. *The Mommy Myth: The Idealization of Motherhood and How It Has Undermined All Women*. New York: Free Press.
Furre, Heidi. 2018. *Dyret*. Roman. Oslo: Flamme forlag.
Frye, Joanne S. 2010. Narrating Maternal Subjectivity: Memoirs from Motherhood. In *Textual Mothers/Maternal Texts*, ed. Elizabeth Podnieks and Andrea O'Reilly. Waterloo, Ontario: Wilfried Laurier University Press.
Grov, Astrid. 2012. Kvinner og cupkakes. (Interview with Toril Moi). *Syn og segn* 2.
Hamm, Christine. 2013. Hva er det med mor? Det ubehagelige moderskapet i norsk samtidslitteratur. In *Kjønnsforhandlinger: Studier i kunst, film og litteratur*, ed. Anne Birgitte Rønning and Geir Uvsløkk. Oslo: Pax forlag.
Hays, Sharon. 1996. *The Cultural Contradictions of Motherhood*. New Haven: Yale University Press.
Isakstuen, Monica. 2018. *Rase*. Roman. Oslo: Pelikanen.
Meyer, Astrid Hygen. 2018. Barselromanene kommer! *Klassekampen*, July 23.
Miller, Tina. 2005. *Making sense of motherhood: A narrative approach*. Cambridge: Cambridge University Press.
Moi, Toril. 2004. Moderskapsmaset. *Morgenbladet*, January 2.
O'Reilly, Andrea. 2010. The Motherhood Memoir and the 'New Momism': Biting the Hand that Feeds you. In *Textual Mothers/Maternal Texts*, ed. Elizabeth Podnieks and Andrea O' Reilly. Waterloo, Ontario: Wilfried Laurier University Press.
Pedersen, Frode Helmich. 2018. Kommentar. *Dagbladet*, August 7.
Ruset, Endre. 2018. Barselbølgen. *Dagbladet*, August 4.
Skomsvold, Kjersti Annesdatter. 2018. *Barnet*. Roman. Oslo: Forlaget oktober.

# Index[1]

[1] Note: Page numbers followed by 'n' refer to notes.

© The Author(s) 2023                                                            171
H. Wahlström Henriksson et al. (eds.), *Narratives of Motherhood
and Mothering in Fiction and Life Writing*, Palgrave Macmillan
Studies in Family and Intimate Life,
https://Doi.org/10.1007/978-3-031-17211-3